BENCHMARKING

A PRACTITIONER'S GUIDE
FOR BECOMING AND STAYING
BEST OF THE BEST

Cover graphic based on "Spider Chart," Chapter 3

BENCHMARKING

A PRACTITIONER'S GUIDE
FOR BECOMING AND STAYING
BEST OF THE BEST

Gerald J. Balm

The Benchmarking Experience
at IBM Rochester

QPMA PRESS

BENCHMARKING:
A Practitioner's Guide for Becoming and Staying Best of the Best

Published by QPMA Press
Quality & Productivity Management Association
300 N. Martingale Road, Suite 230
Schaumburg, Illinois 60173

Publisher: William L. Ginnodo
Publications Manager: Lesley A. Williams
Editor: Kevin C. Shyne

Printed in the United States of America

Printed and bound by McNaughton & Gunn, Inc., Saline, Michigan
Design by The Publishing Services Group, Princeton, Illinois
Cover design by Wildenradt Design Associates, Evanston, Illinois

Copyright © 1992 by Gerald J. Balm

All rights reserved. Except for the usual review purposes, no part of this work may be reproduced or transmitted in any form or by any means—including photocopy, recording, taping, or any information storage and retrieval system—without the written permission of the publisher.

Library of Congress Cataloging-In-Publication Data

Balm, Gerald J., 1936–
    Benchmarking: a practitioner's guide for becoming and staying best of
    the best
    Includes index

ISBN 0-9632167-0-8
1.Total quality management–United States 2. Organizational effectiveness

All inquiries for volume purchases of this book should be addressed to QPMA Press, at the above address. Telephone inquiries may be made by calling 708/619-2909, or by faxing 708/619-3383.

*This book is dedicated to my wife, Rita,
who spent many evenings alone during its preparation;
and to my colleagues at IBM
who gave me the knowledge and encouragement.*

Preface

Benchmarking is a process by which an organization continuously compares its processes, products and services to those of the world's best organizations with the same or similar functions. It is a comparative investigation that analyzes the gap between an organization's present level of performance and the best that exists. Finally, benchmarking is a way to study the methods of "best" organizations, to adapt their ideas, and to become, quickly and efficiently, the best in the world.

Benchmarking is not new. Many companies have used it as a management tool for several decades. But the 1980s witnessed a rebirth of benchmarking in a broader, more dynamic form. Previously, benchmarking referred to competitive analysis, industry analysis, performance benchmarks, functional benchmarks and other traditional (and rather narrowly defined) techniques. These methods are still considered to be benchmarking, but many new elements have been added to the process.

Led by Xerox, IBM, Motorola, 3M and other companies, the re-emergence of benchmarking in a broader form has rekindled interest in its use. Many companies and organizations are finding that benchmarking can become a valuable means of improving their competitiveness and effectiveness. Benchmarking is becoming an integral part of their Total Quality Management system.

This book describes the new, broader and more valuable benchmarking tool and how to apply it in an efficient, effec-

Preface

tive way. The examples are drawn from industry, but the process is equally applicable to education, government, health care, the military and other fields. Wherever organizations are under pressure to improve their processes, products and services, benchmarking offers a practical, affordable tool for becoming the best.

Acknowledgments

The material in this book comes from a variety of sources plus the author's personal experience. A sincere expression of appreciation is sent to the Xerox Corporation, especially to Xerox employees Robert Camp, John Kelsch, and Robert Shattuck. In addition, materials received from Motorola Inc, 3M Company, Kaiser Associates Consultants, and others were helpful. Certainly many of my colleagues in IBM have contributed significantly to the thoughts contained in this book.

Robert Camp's 1989 book, *Benchmarking: The Search for Industry Best Practices That Lead to Superior Performance*, was used heavily to formulate and crystallize many of these thoughts. Frequent references are made to Camp's book because it sets a very firm foundation for contemporary benchmarking concepts. This book builds upon Camp's foundation by adding some things learned in the years since Camp's book was written—and the perspectives from another long-time benchmarking company, IBM. In addition, this author has tried to clarify the closely woven interrelationships of benchmarking, process management, measurement, and project management.

A special thanks go to my colleague, Dan Rourke of IBM Austin, Texas, and to QPMA (Bill Ginnodo and Kevin Shyne) for their many editorial suggestions to make this book more readable and informative.

Also to be acknowledged are Dick Bouquet, Hank Eyrich, and others in the IBM Rochester Computer Integrated Manu-

Acknowledgments

---

facturing group. Chapter 13, "An IBM Rochester Gap Analysis Example," describes some work done by this creative group of benchmarkers.

Contents

1 / Introduction   1

Facing a Global Marketplace   1
The Customer Viewpoint   2
Benchmarking As a Customer Satisfaction Tool   3
Why Benchmarking Now?   4
Some Thought Starters!   5

2 / Background   7

History   7
Preliminary Definitions   8
Goal Setting   8
Coming from Crisis   10
Some Thought Starters!   14

Contents

3 / Definition — 15

Benchmarking General Description — 15
Scope: The New Big "B"! — 23
Targets for Benchmarking — 26
Types of Benchmarking — 31
Some Thought Starters! — 34

4 / Rationale for Benchmarking — 35

Some Reasons for Benchmarking — 35
Some Benefits — 37
The Costs — 38
Return On Investment (ROI) — 38
Some Thought Starters! — 42

5 / What IBM Rochester Did to Facilitate Benchmarking — 43

Prologue — 43
Benchmarking Benchmarking — 47
Top Management Support for Benchmarking — 49
Rochester Site Benchmarking Focal Point Responsibilities — 50
Contacts With External Companies — 56
Future Plans for Benchmarking — 57
Lessons Learned From the Baldrige Application Process — 59
Some Thought Starters! — 62

6 / A Process for Effective Benchmarking — 63

Introductory Comments — 63
Relationship to Process Management, Project Management, and Measurements — 65
Three Additional Process Thoughts — 66
Some Thought Starters! — 68

7 / Subprocess I—Self-Introspection (Process Management) — **69**

Introductory Comments — 69
Step 1—Clarify Customers and Outputs — 71
Step 2—Define Appropriate Measurements — 73
Step 3—Review and Refine the Process Itself — 75
Some Thought Starters! — 78

8 / Subprocess II—Pre-Benchmarking (Preparation) — **79**

Introductory Comments — 79
Step 4—Prioritize/Select What Is to Be Benchmarked — 80
Step 5—Choose Your Benchmarking Partners — 82
Step 6—Set a Level of Data Collection — 87
Some Thought Starters! — 97

9 / Subprocess III—Benchmarking (Execution) — **99**

Introductory Comments — 99
Step 7—Collect the Data and Organize It — 99
Step 8—Calculate Gaps to Baseline — 107
Step 9—Estimate Future Achievement — 109
Some Thought Starters! — 113

10 / Subprocess IV—Post-Benchmarking (Project Management) — **115**

Introductory Comments — 115
Step 10—Present Benchmarking Results — 116
Step 11—Set Goals and Action Plans — 119
Step 12—Implement Actions and Assure Success — 121
Some Thought Starters! — 123

Contents

11 / Subprocess V—Review and Reset (Progress Assessment) — 125

Introductory Comments	125
Step 13—Review Benchmarking Integration	125
Step 14—Assess Project Progress and Update Goals	127
Step 15—Reset Goals and Return to Step 1	128
Some Thought Starters!	131

12 / Some Possible Inhibitors — 133

Introductory Comments	133
Getting Top Management Support	134
Prioritizing What to Benchmark	135
Benchmarking Justification Through ROI Analysis	136
How to Get Started	137
Determining Appropriate Benchmarking Measurements	137
Fear of Breaking Company Security Rules	138
Educating Benchmarking Teams	139
Communicating and Sharing Plans and Results	140
Some Thought Starters!	141

13 / An IBM Rochester Gap Analysis Example — 143

Introductory Comments	143
The CIM Example	144
The Analytical Hierarchy Process (AHP)	145
The Maturity Index (MI)	149
Some AHP/MI CIM Results	153
Some Concluding Remarks	156
Some Thought Starters!	158

14 / Summary and Conclusions — **159**

Summary — 159
Conclusions — 160

Appendix A
Benchmarking Facilitator Responsibilities at IBM Rochester — **163**

Appendix B
Benchmarking Rules of Thumb — **165**

Appendix C
Benchmarking Checklist — **169**

Bibliography — **173**

Books — 173
Booklets and Brochures — 174
Magazine Articles — 174
Other — 175

Index — **177**

Contents

Figures

1. A Benchmarking Motto	12
2. Our Quality Temperature	13
3. Definition of Benchmarking	16
4. Shooting at a Flying Duck	22
5. Prioritization Assistance via "Spider Charts"	30
6. IBM MBNQA Quality Convergence	46
7. Rochester Site Benchmarking Focal Point Responsibilities	51
8. The IBM Rochester Benchmarking Process	64
9. Transfer Function Chart	71
10. A Benchmarking Data Collection Hierarchy	90
11. A Gap Analysis Chart	111
12. AHP Hierarchy of Defined Characteristics	146
13. CIM Hierarchy Example	148
14. CIM Characteristics Ranked by Relative Importance	150
15. Maturity Matrix	151
16. Maturity Index Matrix Definitions	152
17. Early AHP/MI CIM Results	153
18. Another CIM Gap Analysis	153

Tables

1. "Little b, Big B" for Benchmarking	25
2. AHP Pairwise Comparisons and Synthesis	146

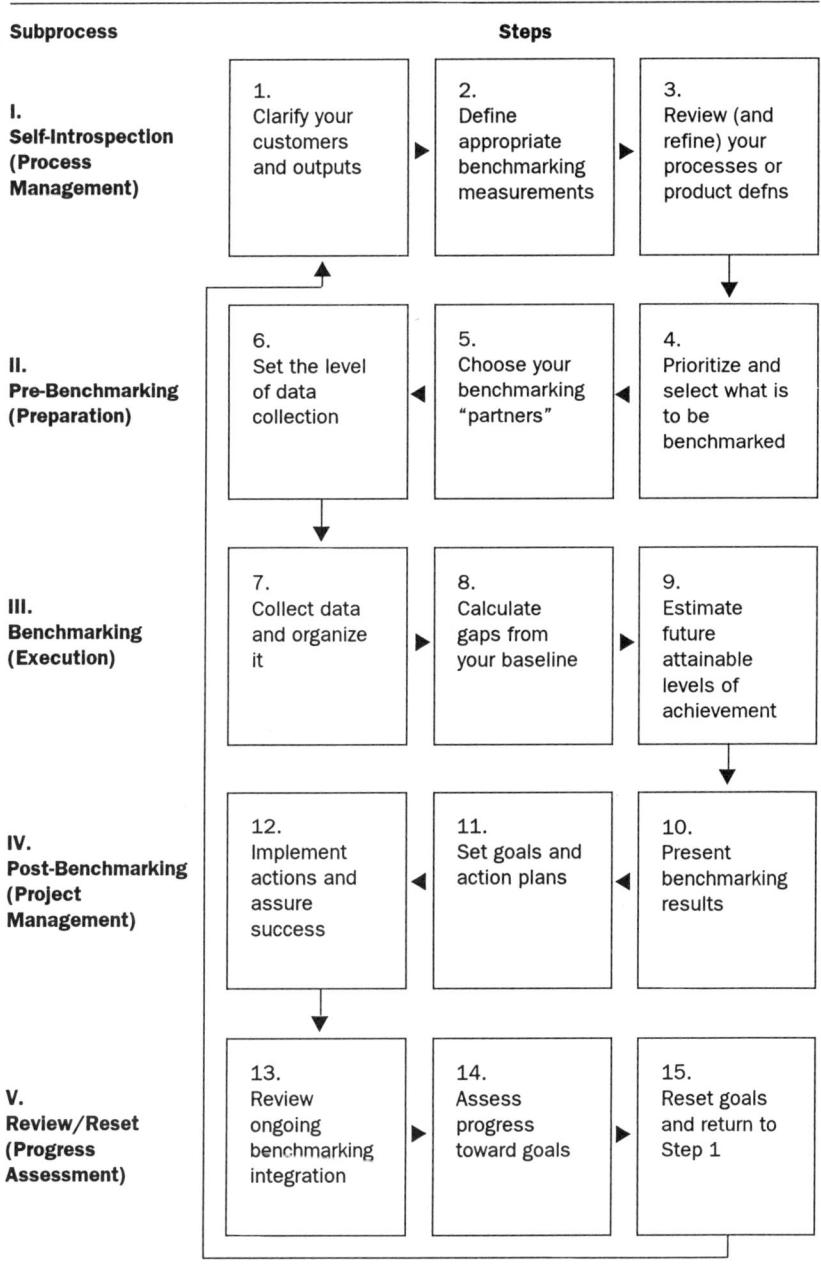

1/Introduction

Facing a Global Marketplace

During the 1970s and 1980s, major segments of American industry were rudely awakened. A new global economy had come into prominence and these American companies found that they were no longer competitive. Quality of offshore products had passed them by, and often at a lower price to the American consumer. What the American public had previously viewed as "junk" or second-rate suddenly had become the product of choice. While it was too late to recover for a few major American industries (e.g., steel, some consumer electronics, etc), other industries (e.g., automobiles, office equipment, etc) awoke in time to fight back.

To be competitive, American industry (re)discovered that it must produce products and services that meet and exceed customer requirements for quality, performance, and function. The price had to be perceived as competitive, and the products and services had to be available to the customer before (s)he purchased them from a competitor. The American public was no longer willing to buy whatever our industry produced at any reasonable price. The fierce loyalty to "buy American" was fading as the gap between American products and offshore products widened. Something had to be done.

Several very important sales concepts, which seemed to have been neglected, were dusted off and given prominence again. Concepts like "the customer is always right" and "highest quality" and "service after the sale" again came into vogue.

The Customer Viewpoint

We now work very hard to produce products and services which provide "total customer satisfaction." Clearly, wherever the word "customer" is used in these discussions, the words taxpayer or voter or student or other forms of consumers and primary stakeholders may be substituted. A very positive customer perception is of high importance. Accurate assessment of customer requirements (at least those in markets we choose to serve) deserves our strong efforts. Customer needs must be prioritized above customer wants or customer desires, but the latter are not to be ignored.

In today's environment, however, customer satisfaction may not be good enough. The term "delighted customers" is coming into prominence. They are customers who are more than satisfied. They are enthusiastic about their purchases. They feel a loyalty toward the producer(s). They even recommend those products and services to friends and colleagues.

As a young design engineer a few years back, this author was taught that the term "defect" referred to "any deviation from the product's functional and performance specification or description." That had clear-cut implications as we designed and manufactured our products to be as defect-free as possible. Recently, many of us have modified our definition of "defect" to mean "any deviation from total customer satisfaction." Now the concept of defect-free products and services has some subtle but very real implications that did not exist under the prior definition. Among other things, it implies a reawakened sense of customer consciousness. It requires stepping out of our own world and looking back at ourselves as our customers do. When we successfully do that, we will often gain a whole new perspective and do our jobs differently.

Benchmarking As a Customer Satisfaction Tool

This "customer satisfaction" mentality has implications for benchmarking—a means by which we can compare our processes, products, and services with the world's best. As discussed later in this book, the measurements and parameters that we use to compare ourselves against others are those which are most important to our customers. In addition, when we determine which other companies (or other internal groups) we want to compare ourselves against, we select these benchmarking partners according to who our customers view as "world class" or "best of breed."

What are some of the other benchmarking results that reflect our drive for defect-free products and services and total customer satisfaction? Certainly, we want to embark on a path of "continuous improvement" toward those goals. One achievement level that we set our sights on is being "best at everything we do." Benchmarking is the tool that tells us not only how good (i.e., what level of achievement) is "best" at this point in time, but it frequently tells us who is currently best and how those best groups were able to accomplish their admirable levels of achievement.

Why Benchmarking Now?

Earlier it was pointed out that worldwide competition is driving many industries toward more extensive use of benchmarking and other quality-improvement tools. It should also be noted that the trend toward benchmarking is enhanced by a new mood and mindset for sharing non-sensitive data across American industry. In recent years, several consortiums involving very unlikely partners have sprung up. Antitrust law permits these arrangements, which are helping more American companies to remain viable in our global economy. In addition, in 1987 the US government enacted the Malcolm Baldrige National Quality Award. The criteria for winning this prestigious award is considered by many companies to be a very effective Total Quality Management (TQM) system. It not only encourages wide use of benchmarking and other quality tools, but also requires that award winners share non-sensitive quality methods and tools with other companies.

Thus, benchmarking appears to be the right tool at the right time. The remainder of this book will describe how to apply this valuable, timely tool to the reader's situation.

Chapter 1: Introduction

SOME THOUGHT STARTERS!

1. Should benchmarking and quality in general be a concern only for companies facing stiff competition in an open market? Should educational institutions, governmental groups, health care, military organizations, and the like also be concerned? Why or why not?

2. Is "customer satisfaction" really the ultimate criteria? Even in a non-competitive situation?

3. How has your business changed over the last few years? Are the processes which produce your products and services the best they can be?

2/Background

History

The earliest recorded references to benchmarking (known to this author) date back many centuries. Military reconnaissance to compare the strength of the enemy to one's own strength and then make strategic and tactical decisions accordingly is a very early application. But this basic idea quickly spread to commercial competitive analysis, sports, politics, some personal relationships (e.g., suitors desiring a beautiful maiden's affections), etc. Indeed, since the earliest recorded history, mankind (and many animals for that matter) have sought ways to avoid situations from which they could not emerge a winner.

Modern commercial benchmarking primarily took the form of competitive analysis, industry analysis, and performance and function comparisons. Like any other valuable tool, unscrupulous practitioners have abused the concept through industrial espionage, insider trading, and other unethical uses. But benchmarking in its straightforward application is an ethical, lawful, and in some cases even necessary tool for survival.

Preliminary Definitions

Before defining benchmarking in more detail, some related definitions are in order. First, the benchmarking tool and concepts are applicable not only to industry but also to government, academe, and any group that wishes to efficiently improve itself. Thus, the term "organization" in this book means any group, subfunction, company, industry, university, governmental unit, etc, that may desire to use benchmarking to improve its efficiency, effectiveness, and/or competitiveness.

Second, the term "benchmarking partner" refers to any group or organization that a benchmarking unit may want to compare itself against. That partner may be another unit within the same company, university, etc, or any group outside the current administration or management. Thus, the term "partner" does not apply to someone within your own benchmarking team, but rather to that other group that has (or hopefully will) agreed to interact with you in a mutually beneficial exchange of information.

Goal Setting

In its simplest form, benchmarking is a means of setting goals or targets. Goal setting can be done in several ways.

The simplest is probably to project desired levels of future achievement based upon extrapolation of past performance. This technique is thoroughly described by many business textbooks as well as by Camp (see Bibliography).

Simple extrapolation is frequently not very challenging for an established organization since it does not account for significant changes like new competition, new technology, higher or lower inflation rates, etc. One could account for these developments by modifying a simple extrapolation of one's performance history. Or one could use "management-mandated" goals (like "zero defects" or more realistically a "six sigma" defect goal) and assume that these will take you to where you want to be. Incidentally six sigma has become quite popular due to many companies benchmarking with Motorola in recent years.

If an organization intends to improve continuously with the ultimate goal of becoming the "best of the best," then there are alternatives. One could use the simple methods described above and hope they will lead to becoming best.

However, benchmarking is the only tool that tells us what "best" means in our measurement system. Benchmarking is the analysis of how good is best and who is best. It also contains an element of the question of "How did these best companies become the best?" Thus, it would seem that the most efficient and effective way to set goals to become best of the best (and thus highly competitive) is to use the benchmarking tool—frequently in combination with some of the other goal-setting tools. Benchmarking can also be used in the context of a "zero defects" approach to quality improvement, as a way of identifying and reducing defects or errors.

Coming from Crisis

All viable organizations want to improve continuously. Most want to become best at what they do (to remain competitive plus to enjoy that admirable childlike pride in being number one). But improvement implies change. Change is OK only when it does not affect me or my job. Human beings have a natural reluctance—indeed almost a fear—to encourage change in their own job. People fear the unknown and usually are more comfortable with the status quo. Change is for those other folks in their organization. How then can a strong motivational desire to be best become part of an organization's very mindset and fabric?

One motivator is crisis. If your company is on a path which will soon take you out of business or necessitate mass layoffs, then it becomes obvious that changing your mindset to become the best by changing your job is preferable to having no job at all (or to degrading the organization to a state of "barely hanging on" which usually means longer hours, fewer benefits, lower or non-existent pay raises, etc.).

Xerox executives have stated that in the late 1970s and early 1980s their competitive position in their marketplace was in crisis. Many of their key financial indicators were disappointing and heading in the wrong direction. Many felt that due to global competition they were on a path which was taking them out of business. But to their credit, the Xerox team put together a Leadership Through Quality emphasis and presented it to their employees and stockholders. Two very important facets of that Leadership Through Quality emphasis pointed out by their CEO David Kearns were Employee Involvement and Benchmarking. In the following decade, Xerox turned around their very tenuous competitive posture. Today the company is again considered to be a formidable competitor which in 1989 won the Malcolm Baldrige National Quality Award.

Even if an organization is not in crisis, can benchmarking help create motivation for it to change (improve) to become the best? Yes it can! My observation as an IBM manager and technical leader is that employees are motivated by several factors. One is fear—fear of losing one's job as described above. But if one's company or organization is doing "pretty well" and is not perceived to be in crisis, an employee's fear of change in his own job may override his fear of loss of the job. Management-mandated goals like six sigma may contain an element of fear (fear of not measuring up to the goal), but also contain an even bigger measure of a second motivator—pride in one's work and loyalty to one's organization. Hopefully, that pride and loyalty will cause all employees to march to the (company) drummer and put out a significant effort to achieve the management-directed goals.

This author believes that use of the benchmarking tool adds another motivational dimension. My observation is that benchmarking generates enthusiasm, motivates employees, and diminishes their natural reluctance toward change. When many employees are given a goal which was derived from benchmarking, they know that someone out there is already achieving that goal and they are motivated to catch up with the best. Their enthusiasm to be able to claim "we're number one" is like the feeling at an athletic contest. The "we can do it if they can do it" syndrome can become a significant motivator.

Figure 1 gives a motto that is particularly pertinent to benchmarking and to my experience at IBM. This author is unable to identify the motto's author, but he heard it first while visiting Milliken & Co. in Spartanburg, S.C., in late 1989.

Figure 1. A Benchmarking Motto

> # Good Is the Enemy of Best, and Best Is the Enemy of Better!

IBM, like many other organizations, is a good company. We are fundamentally sound, employ top-notch employees, and do a lot of things right. Things could always be better, but we view ourselves (and so do many others) as world class in some respects, very good at many others, and good at most of the things we do.

In an organization like this, it is easy to feel that being "good" is good enough. Competition will not permit that attitude. Being content at being "good" may be likened to being content at traveling down a railroad track on a handcar. You're making progress toward your destination (goals) but how long can you ignore that express locomotive (competition) coming up behind you? Will you arrive at your destination? Possibly, if you're already close! Will you remain there safely even if you do arrive first? Not likely!

So, "good is the enemy of best." Benchmarking is the key tool that will tell you what best is, who is already there, and how they got there. But notice the second half of the motto is "... and best is the enemy of better." Clearly, any organization should be working hard at converting its handcar to a sleek new bullet train if it wants to stay ahead.

Figure 2 gives our quality temperature (or health of an organization). This is clearly a case where a little fever could be viewed as good. The best organizations are frequently "hot." Others want to catch the fever to be among the best.

Chapter 2: Background

Figure 2. Our Quality Temperature

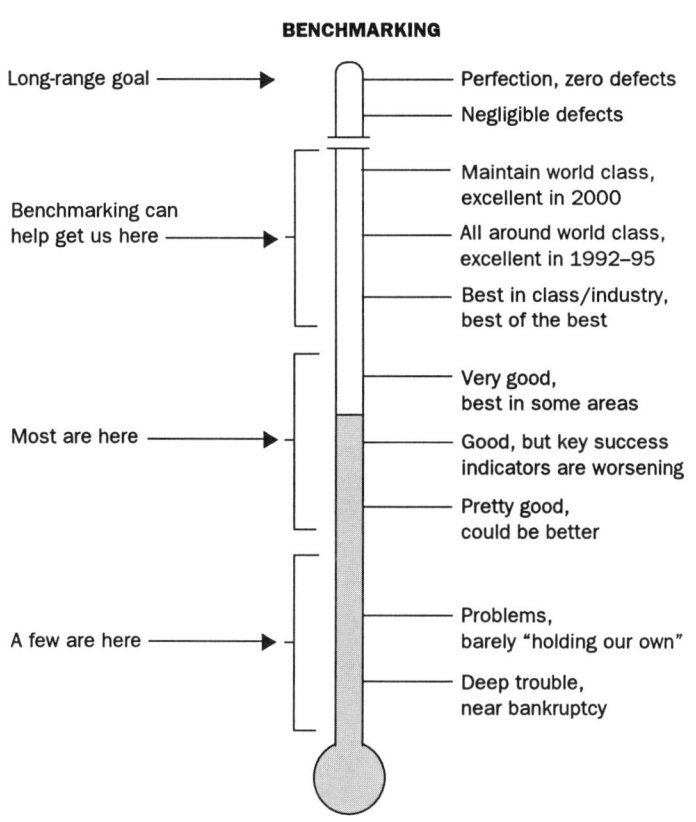

Benchmarking is the process tool to "catch the fever" by borrowing a few of the continuous improvement germs from those world class "hot" organizations.

SOME THOUGHT STARTERS!

1. Why won't many of the traditional management-directive, goal-setting techniques work in this day and age? Or will they?

2. How can an organization which is not in a "change or die" crisis situation motivate itself to strive to be the best at everything?

3/Definition

Benchmarking General Description

Benchmarking can be defined in several ways. Common to all definitions is the idea of goal setting (as described previously). A benchmark is thus a performance or functional goal for achieving an admirable level of quality, performance, cost, and timeliness. Some managers use the terms "benchmarking" and "benchmark" as no more than goal setting and the resultant goal(s).

Many practitioners, including the author of this book, prefer to narrow this very broad "goal setting" definition. See Figure 3 for a summary. That narrowing is achieved by adding the constraint that these lofty goals are determined by

Benchmarking

Figure 3. Definition of Benchmarking

Balm's Definition

The ongoing activity of comparing one's own process, product, or service against the best known similar activity, so that challenging but attainable goals can be set and a realistic course of action implemented to efficiently become and remain best of the best in a reasonable time.

Xerox Formal Definition*

(preferred by former Xerox CEO David Kearns)

Benchmarking is the continuous process of measuring our products, services, and practices against the toughest competitors or those companies recognized as industry leaders.

An Augmenting Xerox Definition*

"The process of consistently researching for new ideas for methods, practices, processes; and of either adopting the practices or adapting the good features, and implementing them to become the best of the best."

---

*From Camp's 1989 Book *Benchmarking: The Search for Industry Best Practices that Lead to Superior Performance.*

---

the ongoing act of comparing one's own process, product, or service against a similar world class ("best") process, product, or service; so that goals can be set and a realistic course of action implemented to become best of the best in a reasonable time frame and then remain the best. Thus, a benchmark goal is one which is set as a result of conducting a valid benchmarking activity.

A formal definition given by Camp and preferred by former Xerox CEO David Kearns is as follows: "Benchmarking is the *continuous process* of *measuring* our products, services, and *practices* against the toughest *competitors* or those companies recognized as industry *leaders*." Another definition from Camp's book which brings an added dimension is that benchmarking is "the process of consistently researching for new ideas for methods, practices, or processes, and of either *adopting* the practices or *adapting* the good features, and implementing them to become best of the best." Each of the italicized words has special significance in these definitions. They are expanded as follows.

First, benchmarking is a *process*. As such, it consists of an ordered sequence of tasks (or steps). You may be benchmarking your own process (or product or service, etc.). But keep in mind that you should be using a benchmarking process to benchmark your target process against world class, comparable processes. This author's proposed benchmarking process is the subject of Chapters 6 through 11 of this book.

Next, benchmarking is a *continuous* process. Too many organizations fall into the trap of using the benchmarking tool only as a short burst of activity just prior to goal-setting time as they prepare next year's operational plan. Then they set it aside for another year until it is time to dust it off and reset the goals. Unfortunately, much has transpired in the company and in those companies or organizations against which it benchmarks. The organization must now try to "catch up" and hope that those other organizations did not do anything significantly different since the last round of benchmarking. As this book explains, there is a hierarchy of levels of benchmarking data collection, ranging from a very low-key monitoring up to a very concentrated comparison that sometimes involves a personal visit to another company's campus. The proposed benchmarking process points out that there is a need for ongoing benchmarking at some appropriate level (usually a lower-keyed level of monitoring) until the organization decides to do another significant, detailed comparison.

Continuing on with the definition description, benchmarking is a continuous process for doing what? The answer is for *measuring* and *comparing*. You select key appropriate measurements (more on this later) and compare yourself to the world's best organizations who do what you do—or in some cases to those organizations who simply have purpose and objectives similar to yours. You analyze the measurement gap between them and your organization in order to set goals to catch up or to stay ahead if you have already successfully become the best.

So you are going to measure and compare. If you have truly set a goal to continuously improve and to become best at everything you do, you will want to measure and compare *all* your products, services, processes, *practices*, procedures, etc. Anything you do or produce that has value-add to the organization (clearly anything that you do or produce that does not have value-add should be quickly questioned and reviewed) is a target for benchmarking. Since most organizations do not have the resources to do full benchmarking on everything they do or produce, targets must be prioritized to determine which demand immediate attention. But even those targets given a medium or low priority need not be relegated to a status of zero benchmarking this year. Lower cost forms of benchmarking in the hierarchy of levels of data collection can be applied. More on target prioritization later.

Next, who will you compare your products, services, processes, etc., against? The answer is not only our direct and toughest *competitors* but against any world class *leader* organization that does what you do. Camp's book very nicely describes how Xerox compared their warehousing and distribution functions against those of the L. L. Bean catalog distribution company. Certainly the L. L. Bean company would not normally be classified as a Xerox competitor, but both clearly need very efficient warehousing and distribution functions. Thus, both learned from each other and benefited from their comparisons.

Finally, the concept of *adopting* or *adapting* beneficial features to one's own organization comes into play. All organizations should feel that they have good employees (or else they should be benchmarking their recruiting and hiring processes as soon as possible). Most of those good employees are creative and innovative, and they frequently have some good ideas for continuous improvement if they are given the opportunity and motivation to make their ideas known. If implemented, these good ideas usually result in continuous improvement. So why do benchmarking? Because in order to become best, you have to know what best is. Secondly, if you can add the creative and innovative ideas of the best organizations (ideas which have often been tested and refined) to those good ideas of your own employees, then you can pick and choose the best combination of ideas to effectively help you become best on the limited resources at your disposal. Implementing only those good ideas coming from your own employees tends to result in business-as-usual incremental improvements. Those are helpful, but sometimes the inbred improvement mentality will not lead you to becoming best—at least not efficiently.

While improvement ideas from within should be encouraged, re-engineering ideas (that is, breakthrough ideas of dramatically different ways of doing things and which lead to dramatic improvements) more often than not come from outside. Application of a new technology that provides a significant improvement would hopefully come from within, but application of an existing, proven technology to a new use (i.e., at your company) resulting in dramatic order-of-magnitude improvement frequently comes from outside.

So, benchmarking will improve the chances of dramatic improvements. That is especially true if you benchmark outside the group of organizations considered to be your competitors. Many organizations have some level of competitive analysis benchmarking already underway which would likely make you aware of any dramatic differences between you and your competitors. Even if there are dramatic differences, your competitors are not likely to share them with you in detail, because that is what gives them their competitive edge in certain functions of their business. However, if you benchmark against non-competitive organizations that share similar objectives to your own organization, they are much more likely to share insights and process details. Thus, broadening your benchmarking scope improves the probability of success.

Before concluding the definition section of this book, there are three more benchmarking terms that should be acknowledged. The term "baseline" alludes to that level of performance which you will use in the near future to compare yourself against for relative improvement. Thus, if you have set a goal to become ten times better within two years, baseline answers the question "Ten times better than what?" You also use it to compare yourself to benchmarking partners and to determine gaps between your performance and that of the best. This level of achievement (i.e., the best you can discover) is called a "benchmark" (the second of the three terms).

A third term is "entitlement." This term has found recent popularity in some circles and stems from the question, What could your customers (external or internal organization customers) be entitled to if all went as well as it could possibly go? Entitlement is a resource-constrained approach to zero defects. In other words, given the resources allocated to the job, what is the best level of accomplishment you could have, assuming no defects, no delays, etc.? Philip Thomas in his recent book about Cycle Time Reduction uses the term entitlement (as well as baseline and benchmark). He defines the above as a "theoretical best" with regards to cycle time. He then proceeds to multiply the theoretical best cycle time by a multiplier to provide a more realistic "entitlement" goal, which he still considers to be very challenging to American industry today. His multiplier factor of the theoretical best cycle time is two to three if the process under analysis is a highly repetitive one (like some manufacturing processes) but would be five to ten in non-repetitive processes (like some service or white-collar tasks). Thus, entitlement is related to benchmarking, because the gap from baseline to benchmark may be compared to the gap from baseline to entitlement. Both are useful for making some very interesting and pertinent observations prior to setting goals for the organization.

These three terms are illustrated in Figure 4. The horizontal axis represents time with a snapshot of performance comparisons taken now and highlighted as a vertical dashed line. The vertical axis represents goodness for any key measurement value. Or, it could represent some weighted average of your key measurements.

In this scenario, looking on the vertical dashed (now-in-time) line, your current performance (baseline) is a solid good. Entitlement would put you into the very good range. The best you can find today (benchmark) is a high very good.

Figure 4 also points out two more interesting ideas. First, entitlement will clearly be higher than baseline (until you operate without any error), but why is benchmark higher than entitlement? How can anyone else do better than zero defects? There are several possible reasons. One possibility is that the benchmark organization has more resources in-

Figure 4. Shooting at a Flying Duck

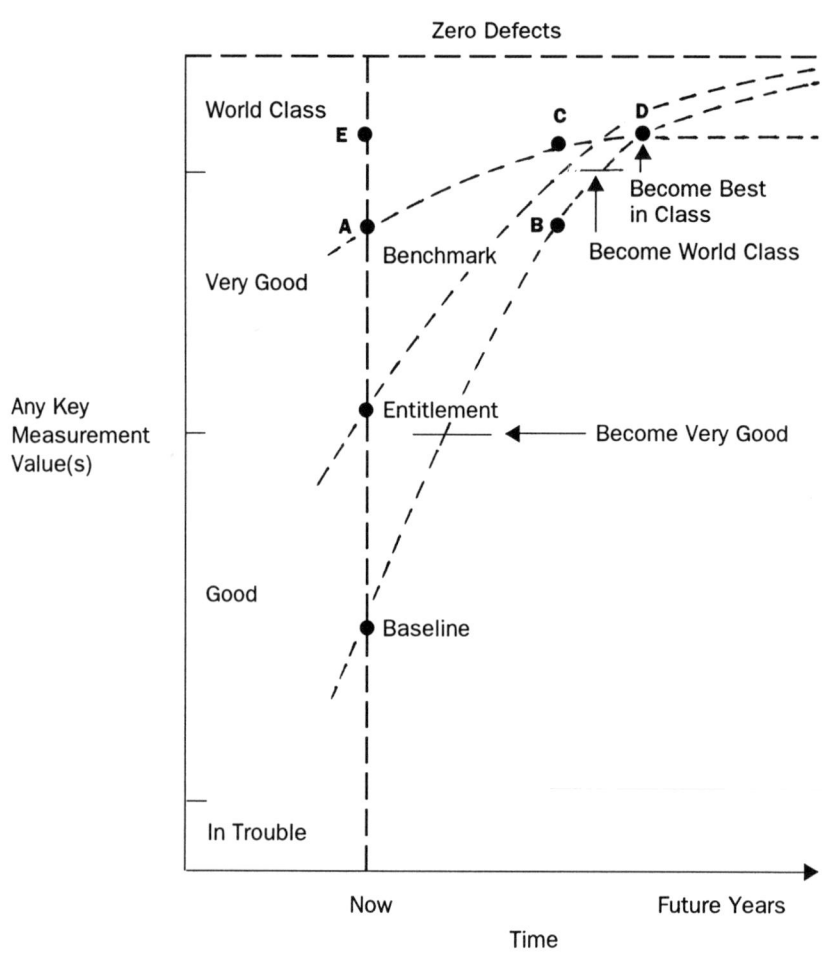

volved and thus is able to out produce you even if you operated at maximum efficiency. Another possibility is that they don't do it the same way you do it. The benchmark organization may have found a more efficient overall process or may have developed more efficient and effective tools and methods. It is this second possible reason that benchmarking will (or will not) demonstrate.

The second interesting idea pointed out by Figure 4 is that the effort to become the best is akin to shooting at a flying duck. If you do a very good job of benchmarking (and entitlement analysis) and compute the gap(s) from baseline, the next task is to eliminate the gap between you and the best. This will require a set of improvements that will raise your achievement level to that of the benchmark (Point A). But of course this improvement does not happen overnight. It takes months (and frequently years) to implement the improvement changes and realize their benefits. Today's benchmark performance (Point A) is actually achieved at Point B.

Have you achieved the goal of becoming best? Absolutely not! Because the benchmarked organization has its own continuous improvement program. It has moved on to Point C. If you told management you would be best when you reached Point B, you have misled them. The actual intercept point where you become best is Point D. You have to implement a program of improvements to reach performance Level E in the indicated time window to become best. This is the reason for the term "shooting at a flying duck." Some clues as to how to do it will be given in the benchmarking process discussion later in this book.

Scope: The New Big "B"!

In 1990, this author developed and taught two benchmarking education classes to over 700 IBM employees. One class was a 1.5-hour Benchmarking Overview class targeted at an audience of IBM managers, process owners, team leaders, and other decision makers. It delved into the "What is it?" and "Why do it?" aspects of benchmarking. A second class was a four-hour Benchmarking Process class for benchmarking team members who would actually be doing benchmarking. This latter class concentrated on the "How do I do it?" and "How do I get started?" aspects. Much of the material from those classes is incorporated into this book.

The subtitle for both classes was "Benchmarking: The New Big B!" Students of the recent re-emphasis on quality in American industry will recall that Juran and other well-known quality experts have expanded the scope of quality from the former "little q" quality of elementary product reliability to the new "Big Q" of overall quality from a much broadened customer viewpoint. In a similar way, others have expanded the idea of the "little c" customer (the person or organization who pays for our product or service) to the newer "Big C" customer which includes all those people along the value-add chain between you and the ultimate consumer. This author proposes a similarly broadened scope of benchmarking (see Table 1) from the former "little b" consisting of internally-driven competitive and industry analysis of our key products and services to a new "Big B" benchmarking.

This new expanded scope of benchmarking is credited to Xerox and a few other companies (including IBM) over the past dozen years. This expanded scope consists primarily of:

- Benchmarking all key processes and practices as well as products and services.

- Making benchmarking comparisons against world class non-competitors (internal and external to your own company) as well as against your top competitors.

- Emphasizing benchmark comparison measures of interest to your customer (both internal and external to your company) as well as traditional "feeds and speeds" metrics.

Chapter 3: Definition

Table 1. "Little b, Big B" for Benchmarking

	Little b	**Big B**
Scope	Products: • Function and Performance • Reliability, Availability, and Serviceability Factors • Competition Comparisons Business/Industry Analysis	All Little b Plus: • All Aspects of Customer Service • All Processes in the Business
Measurements	Related to: • Technology • State of the Art • Nominal Improvements Over Prior Generation	Related to: • Customer Needs • Customer Expectations • Customer Perceptions Internal and External Customers
Targets	Industry/Competition: • Industry Function • Performance • Business Standards	All Little b Plus: • Noncompetitive Companies that Demonstrate Leadership in Processes of Interest

Benchmarking, like any other process tool, has occasionally been misused and misunderstood. The following are some things that benchmarking is NOT:

- A cure for all ills that a struggling organization may be facing
- A means to justify blatant headcount cuts or cycle time reductions

- A one-shot program or activity followed by long periods of total absence of its use
- A process cookbook in which no creativity is needed
- An approved way to conduct industrial espionage on others
- A means to get others to do your work
- A one-way flow of information where you receive and others give
- An improvement tool requiring no cost or effort (but neither must it be too expensive).

Targets for Benchmarking

As was implied in the definition section of this book, the new expanded scope of benchmarking encompasses just about everything you do or produce or sell. Not just products and services, but all processes, practices, critical success factors, customer requirement analyses, etc., become targets for benchmarking. Any key work product used by internal company customers (other employees) as well as by external customers (traditional paying customers) is a target.

Clearly no organization has enough resources to thoroughly benchmark all these targets during a given year. Thus, it must prioritize and spend its limited benchmarking resources on those processes where the potential improvement payback is largest or most critical. Other targets can be benchmarked at a later time or can be benchmarked in a more low-key, resource-conserving manner (e.g., simple research and analysis of public information about a benchmarking partner company without making actual contacts for added detail at this time).

This prioritization of benchmarking targets is sometimes obvious but at other times is very difficult. It is dependent upon the culture of the company or organization, the resources available to benchmarking, the perceived Return On Investment (ROI), the analysis of the cost of not doing benchmarking, and many other factors. But a couple thoughts regarding prioritization are appropriate at this point.

First, the overall value of benchmarking (and thus resources allocated to it) are a direct reflection of the culture/mindset of your company or organization. That mindset is reflected by the management culture and by the attitude of the professionals in the organization. Management negativism or apathy can very quickly kill any enthusiasm for benchmarking. Clear, top-management encouragement is essential or benchmarking will not happen. Even with visible, top-management support, middle and lower line management in many organizations often are perceived by their people as non-enthusiastic. This author's observation is that performance evaluations (and thus merit pay and promotability) of middle and lower line management reinforce the idea that their job is primarily to get the product out on schedule and at planned cost, period! Evaluation criteria like "quality" or "investment for long-term improvement" are often viewed as "nice" but Priority 3 or lower. There is little perceived incentive to encourage the long-term health of the company at these lower management levels. Senior management needs to address this perception, then "walk the talk" to assure it's changed. "Walking the talk" can involve such things as asking about benchmarking at review and planning meetings and requiring benchmarking data as input to strategic plans.

Another management prioritization factor is funding of benchmarking. This author's experience is that senior management should enable benchmarking by providing funds for education and facilitators in competency centers. But the competency centers should not contain money nor manpower for the actual implementation of benchmarking projects. That funding and headcount should come from the functional area's resources so that they feel an ownership and buy-in that does not come from a centralized resource pool. Senior management should, however, insist that their middle and lower line manager's resource plans contain allocations for appropriate benchmarking, just as they should insist on allocations for employee education and training, employee recognition, and the like.

Yet another prioritization factor is the mindset of the organization's professionals. Some professionals believe that to seek out and accept good ideas from other companies is an insult to their own creativity and ingenuity. Most professionals already have several ideas which would improve the organization's output quality and/or efficiency. The standard cry of these folks is "If management would just give me more resources, I could . . . " and usually they are correct. But their ideas are usually what this author calls "business-as-usual" incremental improvements. These improvements typically result in 5 percent or 10 percent or maybe even 15 percent improvement. They are automating some existing process instead of reengineering it. They are removing a 2.5-hour delay time within the process, instead of reorganizing the structure of the organization to remove the two-day delay between one department and the next. Certainly these internally generated improvements should be encouraged, rewarded, and in some cases implemented. But they should be balanced with good improvement ideas from other world class organizations which become known through investment in benchmarking.

Finally, prioritization of benchmarking targets can be assisted by common sense and use of graphical representations. Common sense raises such questions as:

- Where do I think I need the most improvement?
- Where am I the farthest from total customer satisfaction?
- What process improvements offer high potential rewards, but require relatively low investment of resources?
- What aspects of my organization produce the highest-per-unit defects?
- Where do the big delays or bottlenecks appear to be?

Graphical representations can be useful attention-getters, such as the Spider Chart depicted in Figure 5. While a chart like this is more useful following benchmarking, you probably have a pretty good idea of where you are (baseline) and where the really good companies are (benchmark) and what your customers really want (customer satisfaction). Benchmarking will validate some of your perceptions and make them more accurate and defendable. It will also frequently give you some surprises when you do good effective benchmarking. It will occasionally shock you with some real revelations and breakthroughs. But you can use pre-benchmarking perceptions coupled with good graphics to point out perceived key gaps that will help in setting priorities. The scenario depicted by Figure 5 is interpreted as follows.

Eight key measurements (or eight key benchmarking target process results) are shown in Figure 5. The center of the circle is the worst value imaginable for each process or measurement. The radius of the circle normalizes each process or measurement so that its value at the circumference represents total customer satisfaction. Thus, the values assigned to the inner and outer point of each measurement may well

Figure 5. Prioritization Assistance via "Spider Charts"

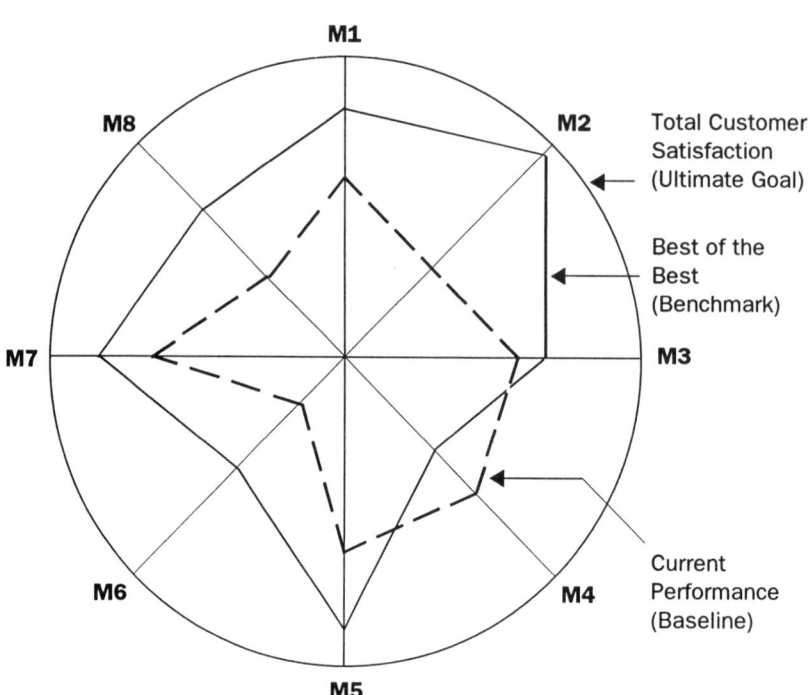

M1, M2, . . . , M8 are Eight Key Measurements of Interest

be different from the corresponding values for other measurements. But each measurement radius represents the range from "terrible" to total customer satisfaction.

One can quickly tell several things from a graphic like this. For example, Measurements 5 and 7 appear to be in reasonable shape—the baseline is not far behind benchmark nor total customer satisfaction. Measurement 4 indicates that the organization is already best-of-breed benchmark although it has a ways to go to attain total customer satisfaction. But Measurement 6 is more troublesome. It indicates a very large gap to customer satisfaction although the benchmark in this case is not too far ahead of the organization's performance. But even worse, Measurement 2 shows a huge gap between current performance and total customer satisfaction, and the fact that somebody out there (the benchmark) is doing a lot better. Given the information contained in this diagram, one might well prioritize Measurement 2 (or process) as demanding immediate attention followed closely by Measurement 6 (or process).

Clearly, one would want to update this diagram after benchmarking. The same graphic technique can be used to depict the findings of a benchmarking activity, not just perceptions before the fact. And certainly one should not dismiss other graphic techniques like Pareto charts, fishbone diagrams, control charts, curve-fitting methods, etc. Common sense tells us to use what fits the individual situation.

Types of Benchmarking

There are several distinct types of benchmarking in common use today. This section will briefly describe five types. Camp's book describes the first four and briefly mentions the fifth. They are included here for completeness and to express this author's thoughts on each.

- **Internal Benchmarking**—Comparing yourself against a similar process, product, or service within your own organization (not necessarily at your location). Potential benchmarking partners (the other units you wish to share data with) are easier to identify. Sharing company confidential data should be easier. You are less likely to find substantial improvement differences. But this type should generally be considered first.

- **Competitive Benchmarking**—Comparing yourself against the toughest external competitive organization(s). They are usually easy to identify and are slightly more likely to have significant improvement differences. However, they are less likely to share them with you (especially sensitive data—which shouldn't be shared without appropriate agreements anyway). Real breakthrough discoveries are rare. If you have been "keeping your eye on the competition," you would have noticed their strengths long ago. This type should be standard fare.

- **Functional Benchmarking**—Comparing yourself against other world class companies who do what you do. They are often in the same general industry (e.g., electronics) but are not direct competitors. Examples for IBM might be Xerox or Motorola. They are more likely to share data (even if it's sensitive) than direct competitors. They are also a little more likely to have substantial improvement differences, but it will be a little harder to identify them.

- **Generic Benchmarking**—Comparing yourself to a world class company that is not even in your industry but that does some processes similar to yours (e.g., the recruiting process). Examples for IBM might be Milliken & Company or Cadillac. These companies are often harder to identify, but are more likely to share extensive data and are more likely to have a substantial improvement difference, even a technology or methodology breakthrough (especially if the process you want to compare is a critical one to them). Opportunities of this type should be sought, but limited resources might lead you to other types where the probability of applicable ideas is usually greater.

- **Consultant Study Benchmarking**—Comparing yourself to any other world class company by utilizing the contracted services of a consultant. The major advantage of this method is that the consultant can act as an independent, neutral third party to collect and analyze sensitive data (reporting only averages, ranges, trends, or other non-sensitive forms of data) without diverting human resources from your company. This type is often useful coupled with competitive benchmarking. The downside is that you must pre-educate the consultant on what you want, then pay for the study although the results must frequently be shared with other organizations as an inducement for their participation.

SOME THOUGHT STARTERS!

1. What are the advantages and disadvantages of making benchmarking a continuous process in your organization?

2. Should the benchmarking scope be broadened to the new "Big B" benchmarking in your organization? Why or why not?

3. When choices must be made due to resource limitations, what are the reasons for prioritizing some processes, products, or services ahead of others to receive immediate benchmarking attention?

4. What is the right ratio of "generic benchmarking" to other types of benchmarking in your organization at this time? Will it change as time passes and conditions change?

5. What resources do you have available for benchmarking?

6. Will senior management support a benchmarking effort?

4/Rationale for Benchmarking

Some Reasons for Benchmarking

There is a wide spectrum of reasons to benchmark your activity against world-class organizations. One very basic yet extremely important reason was mentioned earlier in this book. If your quality improvement strategy includes the goal of becoming best at everything you do, then benchmarking is the only way to find out when and if you achieve that goal. It is the only tool that really tells you how good is best. If done effectively, it will also tell you who is now best, and it should tell you what they do that results in this admired level of achievement. Going into more detail, the spectrum of reasons for benchmarking include:

Benchmarking

- The organization is in a life or death crisis situation.
- The organization is in trouble and management is pushing hard for total quality.
- The organization is still viable, but competition is growing stronger and key company indicators are worsening.
- The organization needs some big breakthrough improvements to remain competitive.
- The organization needs to benchmark to fulfill its total quality management plans (e.g., Baldrige Award criteria).
- The organization needs more improvement ideas to supplement those of its own employees.
- The organization has a casual but sincere interest to see how it stacks up.
- A unit of the organization needs to impress top management.
- The organization has some idle time and has nothing better to do.

Hopefully, your organization is not benchmarking for the reasons at either end of this spectrum. The key reasons in this author's mind would be:

- To find out where you measure up as a world class organization.
- To help identify your strengths (to reinforce them) and your weaknesses (to treat them as real opportunities for improvement).
- To learn from leadership experience of others.
- To assist you in justifying and prioritizing resource allocation toward improvements.

- To enable you to remain competitive and to achieve total customer satisfaction.

Some Benefits

The preceding reasons for benchmarking suggest some of the more obvious benefits:

- Improvement of key financial (and other) indicators.
- Remaining viable, competitive, and profitable.
- Incorporation of industry best practices into the organization.
- Establishment of credible and effective goals.
- Improvement of definition of customer requirements.
- Becoming/staying a leader.
- Identifying strengths and weaknesses.
- Faster, lower-risk attainment of challenging goals.
- Access to creative thinking of employees of benchmarking partner companies.
- Added credibility for your own improvement process.

Some other perhaps more subtle benefits are as follows:

- Justification of potential break-through improvements.
- Becoming the best that you can be.
- Cross-pollination of good ideas across industries.
- Establishment of professional interactions and contacts.
- Reduction of employee reluctance to change.
- Improvement in employee morale and pride.

Benchmarking

The benefits to any one organization depend upon a number of factors related to its particular situation. However, effective benchmarking will always result in some combination of these benefits.

The Costs

Since nothing is free in this world, what is the downside of benchmarking? What are the costs? Some potential costs are as follows:

- Some resources (training, research, preparation, and data collection) must be expended to benchmark.
- There is risk of inadvertent and unintended sharing of confidential information.
- There is cost to implementing the discovered improvements.
- In larger organizations, there will be a cost to coordinate the effort.

It should be noted that these costs are in reality investments in the future. As in all other business investments, if they don't pay a dividend in the future, their implementation cannot be justified.

Return on Investment (ROI)

Some managers have asked "How can I assure a good return on the investment I might make in benchmarking?" This author's response is, "There is no absolute assurance. But can you afford not to do benchmarking?"

If you don't benchmark, the result will probably be implementation of a few good ideas from within your organization that produce business-as-usual incremental improvements. That accomplishes the goal of continuous improvement. But does it put you on the path of becoming the best? Probably not. Many of the best organizations use benchmarking and thus have the good ideas of other best organizations to augment the good ideas from their own employees. Thus, their improvement curves typically are steeper than a business-as-usual incremental improvement curve. A non-benchmarking organization would never be able to catch up. Business as usual will not make you world class, nor will it keep you there if you are fortunate enough to have reached that level. But since non-benchmarking organizations will probably never know how good is best or who is currently best and why, they may feel very content.

If a manager does decide to do some benchmarking but allocates such meager resources that it must be done poorly (e.g., little preparation, haphazard selection of benchmarking partners, etc.), the results will be less than effective. Trips taken to visit benchmarking partners will produce what this author calls "interesting visits" rather than a truly effective benchmarking activity. On an interesting visit, you will probably learn a few things of value, but the ROI is usually marginal.

At the other extreme, if you decide to follow the process for benchmarking suggested in this book (or as suggested by Camp or others) but allow yourself to get bogged down in the early stages, you may increase your investment to such a high level that it would take the discovery of a huge breakthrough to achieve a favorable ROI.

Experience has taught this author that common sense and overall balance will maximize ROI on benchmarking, just as it does in so many other management decisions. Benchmarking must be treated like any other risk-taking investment betting on a future return. There are methods (using a number of assumptions) to calculate a metric ROI for an investment in employee education and training. There are also methods to calculate ROI on the purchase of a new piece of capital equipment. To calculate an ROI on benchmarking often requires similar techniques (and many similar assumptions) and some creativity.

Again, this author's experience has led him to believe that common sense, balance, and a dash of faith will usually create enough ROI justification so that accounting techniques are unnecessary. In addition, when numeric methods are attempted, two major problems frequently arise: 1) the benchmarking team did not keep good records on resources expended directly on benchmarking and that would not have been expended for other reasons (i.e., investment), and 2) management frequently couples improvements learned from benchmarking with improvements from in-house ideas and from other sources (like a new technology). The improvements measured are attributable to several reasons, and management cannot sort out and isolate improvements due solely to benchmarking (i.e., return). This author feels that these two "problems" are not really problems at all. Again, good common sense and management judgment can tell, intuitively, if it was worth it. Usually everyone is satisfied except maybe a few finance folks. The organization's management can still manage by facts. It's just that the calculations of investment and return are done at a higher level which combines benchmarking with other improvements. This author (an old design engineer) pleads that organizations be careful not to allow the resources needed to calculate benchmarking ROI to eat up a significant part of the benchmarking ROI.

One last point on benchmarking ROI is an answer to the question "Can a benchmarking activity (investment) be successful even if no improvement changes result?" The answer is "Yes, but it depends on the reason(s)!" If the reason is because the organization did not select an appropriate world class benchmarking partner or did not prepare properly for the information exchange or both (this happens more often than this author would like to admit, frequently because of impatience and lack of education), then the only thing that can be salvaged from the experience is the lesson learned and the determination to do better next time. But if the reason for no applicable or implementable ideas is because the organization is just plain as good as or even better than the world class partner, then it has benefited significantly. The organization has learned how good world class is and that it has achieved this level or better.

SOME THOUGHT STARTERS!

1. What are the more important reasons for your organization to increase its benchmarking activity and/or effectiveness? What reasons would argue against it?

2. Does your organization have the patience and faith to wait months (possibly years) for the benchmarking ROI to show up in your bottom-line measurements?

5/What IBM Rochester Did to Facilitate Benchmarking

Prologue

IBM has a long tradition of striving for quality and excellence in everything it does. It hires well-trained, creative employees who are empowered and encouraged to use the latest technologies and techniques to create and produce high quality products, services, and processes. It fosters an environment of employee contribution and participative management. Most IBM observers would say that it does a lot of things right.

However, IBM found itself in the same dilemma as many other U.S. companies over the past few decades. Strong global competition was eroding its market share. Other key financial indicators were declining or not meeting expectations of industry analysts. Competition for its products and services was gaining ground.

Thus, the 1980s saw a reawakening of some very long-term and basic values at IBM. We were not yet in crisis, but we recognized that we had to change or we would soon find ourselves in a crisis situation. We tried several quality re-emphasis programs, and while each produced substantial benefit, each of them lost momentum after a time and a business-as-usual mentality returned.

In the mid-1980s, the U.S. government (with a lot of help from private industry) decided that it was time to provide a stimulus for U.S. industry to regain some lost worldwide competitiveness. The Japanese government had successfully utilized a highly-regarded national quality award called the Deming Award (named after U.S. quality guru W. Edwards Deming) to stimulate its industry to higher levels of quality and worldwide competitiveness. Was the United States of America so proud and so myopic that it could not benchmark this world class success and apply it to its own situation? Thankfully, the answer was "NO"!

In 1987 the U.S. Congress passed legislation to create the Malcolm Baldrige National Quality Award (MBNQA) named after a former Secretary of Commerce who had been killed in a tragic accident. The criteria for winning this award were derived by a group of U.S. industry quality leaders working with the Department of Commerce. This set of criteria evolved into a very comprehensive Total Quality Management (TQM) system. The award competition was launched in 1988.

IBM reviewed the MBNQA criteria and found them to be a worthy basis for its quality emphasis. The resulting TQM system collected and focused much of IBM's prior quality programs into a cohesive and comprehensive model. Thus, IBM quickly decided to participate in the MBNQA competition.

Chapter 5: What IBM Rochester Did to Facilitate Benchmarking

However, to marshal the resources needed to create a very competitive application for IBM-U.S. would be a huge undertaking. IBM-U.S. is a very large company (over 200,000 employees) consisting of several distinct business units. So, a decision was made to not implement the MBNQA criteria throughout the company, but to select a single functional unit to enter the official competition.

The IBM facility at Rochester, Minnesota has been highly regarded by top management as a leader in many quality aspects. However, the year 1988 was an extremely busy one for IBM Rochester, due to the announcement of their new AS/400 computer system. So it removed itself from consideration to enter the MBNQA competition that year. But it did start a self-assessment using the criteria.

In late 1988 and early 1989, IBM Rochester readied itself for a run at the MBNQA. It was selected by Corporate Management to officially apply and the application team was assembled. In the meantime, by using the criteria for a year, IBM-U.S. (and specifically IBM Rochester) had discovered an interesting convergence. Figure 6 demonstrates this very nicely. Starting in the upper left corner of the figure, IBM's three very fundamental, unchanging, long-term "Basic Beliefs" are stated. These beliefs are implemented (as you move left to right in the figure) through a set of market-driven quality principles and initiatives to the set of six "Critical Success Factors" that IBM Rochester had selected to emphasize. Now look at the seven Malcolm Baldrige National Quality Award criteria categories in the lower left of the figure. They evolve through some Quality Operating Principles (note that benchmarking is one of the principles) and converge very nicely into our six Critical Success Factors. We knew we were on the right track.

This author believes that the organizations represented by many of this book's readers could discover (or have dis-

Figure 6. IBM MBNQA Quality Convergence (IBM Source Unknown)

IBM Basic Beliefs Quality Values
- Respect for individual
- Service to customer
- Excellence in execution

MD Quality Principles
- Understand markets
- Commit to leadership
- Excellence in execution
- Customer is final arbiter

MD Quality Initiatives
- Customer satisfaction
- Defect elimination
- Cycle time reduction
- Employee participation
- Closed loop quality/mgmt system

Rochester Critical Success Factors
- Implement requirements definition
- Enhance total product strategy and plans
- Six-sigma defect reduction
- Cycle time reduction
- Participative management
- Excellence in education

MBNQA Evaluation
- Leadership
- Info & analysis
- Planning
- Human resources
- Quality assurance
- Quality results
- Customer satisfaction
  – Approach
  – Deployment
  – Results

Quality Operating Principles
- Continuous improvemt closed loop
- Customer focused
- Mgmt by fact
- Mgmt involvement
- Prevention based
- Defect elim
- Processes
- Self-eval
- Particip mgmt
- Knowledge
- Supplier invol
- Benchmarking
- Teamwork

Chapter 5: What IBM Rochester Did to Facilitate Benchmarking

covered) a similar convergence. The point of this discussion is this thought: pick a good Total Quality Management system, integrate and converge it with your organization's quality efforts, and "just do it!" Incidentally, if benchmarking is not a part of the resulting implementation plan, review the plan for completeness.

Benchmarking Benchmarking

As was stated in the preceding section, IBM Rochester applied for the Malcolm Baldrige National Quality Award (MBNQA) in 1989. The entire site (about 8,000 employees) worked very hard starting in late 1988 in order to assemble the application document and submit it by the April 1989 deadline. It was difficult to condense all we knew and did into the application's page limit.

In that very busy 4- to 5-month Baldrige application writing period, we learned a lot of things about ourselves. Some of those things were already on our "to be fixed" list. Others we knew subconsciously but had chosen not to surface. A couple were mild surprises. None were really shockers. We compiled a list of our shortcomings (we called them our "warts" after benchmarking Xerox and finding they had used that very descriptive term). We prioritized those warts (for resource allocation purposes) and we assigned "owners" to them (the owner is responsible for seeing that the wart is removed or reduced to insignificance).

One of the warts IBM Rochester discovered in early 1989 pertained to benchmarking. IBM has a long history of benchmarking and has done it very well. We were probably a pioneer benchmarking company as it pertains to some narrow (traditional) benchmarking activities like competitive analysis, computer industry analysis, and performance and functional comparisons against top competitors using "benchmark computer workloads." But, IBM had allowed itself to become a little complacent.

In that 1989 MBNQA application writing effort, IBM Rochester discovered another benchmarking-related wart. While our site had several very competent (but traditional) benchmarking activities as ongoing assignments, these activities were in isolated pockets spread across our organization. There was no single manager on site (several of the site's senior managers report to Directors and Vice Presidents at Headquarters) to whom all these benchmarking activities reported. As a consequence, no one person was constantly aware of all the site's benchmarking activity. Thus, no one could spot the gaps (unfulfilled needs) of our benchmarking. We were doing a good but incomplete benchmarking job.

In mid-1989, IBM Rochester was pleased to learn that it had been selected by the MBNQA's examiners as a finalist. We would receive a site visit to confirm the information in our application. That site visit by a small team of Baldrige examiners took place in the fall of 1989. Their feedback corroborated our wart list including our need for more comprehensive benchmarking.

About the time that the Baldrige team corroborated IBM Rochester's benchmarking wart, this author was returning from an IBM Community Service Assignment (a paid leave of absence to work on a local community need). Because of my over 20 years of IBM experience in Development (where I had done some benchmarking) and in Technical Education, I was assigned to re-enter IBM in a small site Quality group. One of my initial assignments was to fix the benchmarking wart.

I started by benchmarking the process of benchmarking. At that time, I was not aware of a benchmarking process like the one proposed in this book. I analyzed the benchmarking situation of IBM Rochester and started searching for benchmarking best organizations. Quickly Xerox (and Robert Camp's 1989 Benchmarking book) surfaced. Other companies came to light, including Motorola, 3M, and my own IBM. Some consultant firms with benchmarking expertise also popped out. Armed with this information, I was off and running.

Top Management Support for Benchmarking

With the knowledge of benchmarking at IBM Rochester and of the activities of some world class benchmarking organizations, I proposed in mid-January 1990 some recommendations to the IBM Rochester Site Quality Steering Committee. This committee was composed of most of the site's senior management team and chaired by Site General Manager Larry Osterwise. While some of the committee members reported directly to Headquarters, Larry Osterwise was the Senior Manager on site and the "landlord" of the site's facilities.

In my mid-January 1990 presentation to the Site Quality Steering Committee, I recommended two major items. First was the creation of a Site Benchmarking Focal Point responsibility, and the second was the appointment by each of the site's senior managers of a knowledgeable benchmarking representative from their respective groups to serve on a Site Benchmarking Council to be chaired by the Benchmarking Focal Point. The Site Quality Steering Committee accepted my recommendations, assigned the Focal Point responsibility to the site Quality Group (so I was the natural appointee), and asked me to document to each of them (for their review and action) a list of Focal Point responsibilities and an official request for a Council appointee along with that position's responsibilities. Both the Focal Point and Council members duties will be described later in this chapter.

Within a couple days, I complied with the Quality Steering Committee's request. I sent them each a proposed list of Benchmarking Focal Point responsibilities (described in Appendix A, "Benchmarking Facilitator Responsibilities at IBM Rochester"), and formalized the request for Benchmarking Council representatives from each of their organizations. A short time later, their responses were returned to me with some minor refinements, clarifications on the Focal Point responsibilities and a Council representative's name.

Even before most of the Quality Steering Committee members responded, Larry Osterwise took his copy of my proposal/request and forwarded it to his direct-report functional managers with his handwritten note on the margin. He asked each of them to work with me (the Focal Point) on the request. In addition he asked each of them to submit to me within two months (by late March) their area's plan for 1990 benchmarking activity so that I could summarize those plans to him. He further asked those senior managers to ensure that their plans included at least one completed benchmarking activity within six months (by late July). I forwarded Larry's requests to the other site senior managers (who reported to Headquarters rather than to Larry) and received their cooperation as well. With top management support like that, IBM Rochester was destined to become a world class benchmarking organization very rapidly.

Rochester Site Benchmarking Focal Point Responsibilities

Figure 7 summarizes the responsibilities for the IBM Rochester Site Benchmarking Focal Point. These responsibilities will be described in more detail in the following paragraphs. But some general comments are in order first. One comment

Chapter 5: What IBM Rochester Did to Facilitate Benchmarking

Figure 7. Rochester Site Benchmarking Focal Point Responsibilities

- Help Identify High-Potential Opportunities
- Conduct Appropriate Benchmarking Studies
- Maintain a Benchmarking Data Base
- Develop/Teach/Broker Classes
- Be a Benchmarking Competency Center
- Act as a Site Consultant
- Assist IBM Headquarters with Benchmarking
- Communicate Results to Site Benchmarking Council
- Coordinate Site Contacts to Motorola, Xerox, others

is that this benchmarking focus could have been implemented organizationally by moving all the ongoing benchmarking activities under a single manager. This method was considered and rejected because in many cases there were good reasons to have activities report where they were. In addition, we wanted to encourage all functional groups to do their own benchmarking. Also, IBM traditionally changes organizational structures as needed. To depend on an organizational structure focus for benchmarking seemed less desirable than a functional structure focus. Finally, smaller companies may feel that they cannot afford a Focal Point. That assignment does not have to be full-time, and help is now available by benchmarking best companies. Again, the question should be, "Can we afford not to have a Focal Point?"

The first two responsibilities indicate a need for the Focal Point to work with site management to help them identify and prioritize benchmarking candidates. But note that the second responsibility indicates that the Focal Point actually conducts only a few "appropriate" benchmarking activities. In most cases, (s)he assists and facilitates subject matter experts from the functional areas as they do the benchmarking. Their expertise is critical to the success of the benchmarking activity, and it is generally easier to teach a subject matter expert the process for doing effective benchmarking than it is to teach a benchmarking expert the needed subject matter expertise. In addition, IBM Rochester did not centralize a pool of money or people to do benchmarking. We believe this tool will be better integrated into the mindset and fabric of functional areas easier if they must incorporate it into their planning and budgeting rather than tapping some benchmarking competency center to do it all for them. The "appropriate" benchmarking activities that a Focal Point might do are those for which (s)he is qualified and that are of a general nature (e.g., employee recognition programs to honor top quality contributors).

The responsibility to maintain a benchmarking data base is an important one. Who else but the Focal Point has a broad awareness of who is benchmarking what processes (or is planning to do it) against whom and when? This centralized repository of benchmarking information is important for two reasons. The first is to share the information between interested groups in your company or organization so that they do not duplicate each other's work and so that the benefits of any benchmarking activity are spread as widely as possible. The second reason is to prevent multiple groups in your company or organization from wasting the time of popular benchmarking partners by asking the same questions over and over, thus creating an image that your groups do not even talk to each other. IBM Rochester had defined a benchmarking database format and was searching for an appropriate computer data base tool when it became obvious that what we needed was bigger than a Rochester database—it was a total IBM data base. So we escalated the need (and our research) to IBM Headquarters, which is discussed later in this section.

Chapter 5: What IBM Rochester Did to Facilitate Benchmarking

Like a data base, the responsibility to develop and teach (or act as a broker for) benchmarking education classes was quickly cited as a need. We surveyed the availability of existing classes and found none existed within IBM. Outside IBM, a few classes available to the public were offered by Motorola, Kaiser Associates Consulting firm, and a few others. But these classes did not appear to meet the IBM Rochester requirements or were deemed to be rather expensive. So, as discussed earlier, two local Rochester benchmarking classes (an overview and a how-to process course) were developed and taught. As in the case of the benchmarking data base, this work was also passed up to Headquarters. The need was clearly broader than for IBM Rochester employees. Incidentally, the IBM Rochester benchmarking classes were benchmarked against the existing internal Xerox benchmarking classes by a two-way sharing of class content with a Xerox education manager, and improvements were made as a result.

The next two responsibilities (benchmarking competency center and site benchmarking consultant) were a natural outgrowth of a strong need for help by site benchmarking teams. Also, the Focal Point had been given the opportunity to benchmark benchmarking and thus had built up a certain proficiency level. These responsibilities (along with teaching the benchmarking classes) are felt to be very important and have a high return on investment. By getting the many decision makers and benchmarking teams off to an efficient and effective start, the quality of benchmarking is improved and the resources spent on a Focal Point are returned to the organization with a large multiplier. Again, as word of IBM Rochester's competency in benchmarking got around the company, that consulting responsibility spread to Headquarters and to many other IBM locations around the world.

Benchmarking guidance to IBM Headquarters as a Focal Point responsibility has already been mentioned. Examples were the need for a benchmarking data base and for education classes. Benchmarking talks were given at several IBM locations and at Headquarters. Robert Camp's benchmarking book (over 600 copies) was distributed at local classes and to interested IBM employees throughout the world. Likewise, copies of the local Rochester benchmarking class handout package were sent to IBM requestors around the world. An "IBM Rochester Benchmarking Experiences and Recommendations" report (including the proposed benchmarking checklist and the rules-of-thumb list in this book's appendix) was also distributed to IBMers far and wide. In addition, IBM Rochester hosted the first (of what is now a semi-annual) IBM Benchmarking Conference in October 1990. Again, credit goes to Xerox for improvement ideas for this conference. I benchmarked my plans against their established conferences. Similarly, corporate-wide benchmarking communication vehicles like an electronic forum (now implemented), a newsletter (not yet implemented), a coordinator's network (now implemented), and other ideas were suggested. So, in net, the Rochester Focal Point, due to early development of benchmarking expertise to fix a Baldrige Award criteria wart, has shared that expertise throughout IBM (as well as some sharing with a few IBM customers and at some benchmarking conferences outside IBM).

The responsibility of chairing the Site Benchmarking Council is also a high priority. As described earlier, these representatives from the site's major functional areas are the eyes, ears, and voice of the Focal Point across the site. Recent benchmarking news (e.g., new classes, what Headquarters is doing, recent significant benchmarking projects, etc.) is shared with all site benchmarking teams and management through representatives. They also keep the Focal Point aware of needs and recent benchmarking findings or changes implemented. At Rochester, the Council is the Focal Point's source of information on benchmarking plans and activity. Twice a year, the Focal Point summarizes to site senior management what benchmarking has been happening in the trenches based on input from this team. (Interestingly, the Focal Point asks two questions: "What benchmarking has occurred in the last six months?" and "What is being changed as a result of that benchmarking?") Once a year, about mid-February, the Focal Point summarizes to senior management the benchmarking plans across the site for that calendar year based upon team input. In addition, this team of benchmarking-literate folks serves as a sounding board to critique the Focal Point's new plans and proposals. They are valuable indeed.

The final listed responsibility is to coordinate site contacts with popular non-IBM benchmarking partner companies like Xerox and Motorola. This was found to be necessary because several different functional area groups were using various means to establish contacts in parallel. By funneling those contacts through an IBM Rochester Focal Point, who in turn established a single entry into the partner companies, much more efficient communications were established—to the delight of both IBM and the partner. In addition, several managers and senior technical people were seeking a way to attend public quality seminars offered by certain other companies. The Focal Point established a common contact to enroll these folks in the seminars (and also encouraged other managers to attend).

One final responsibility added to the list in early 1991 (after IBM Rochester won a 1990 Baldrige Award) was to take the lead in defining the process to efficiently handle the many incoming requests from organizations that wanted to benchmark with us (or just chat with a local "expert" on some topic). This process had to minimize the impact on the site's technical experts who had to concentrate on normal company business and on continuous improvement. The process also had to give a high-quality, timely response to the requestors. This was (and still is) a challenging balance.

Contacts with External Companies

IBM has facilitated communications within the company since its beginnings. Employees are encouraged to talk to one another about common needs and interests. A worldwide IBM electronic mail system and phone system with a user-friendly electronic phone book are available to all employees. Other communication mechanisms like an internal Technical Report system and an Interdivisional Technical Liaison (ITL) system are in place. The Technical Reports (and shorter Technical Memos) are entered into an easy-to-use and readily accessible data base called the IBM Technical Information Retrieval Center (ITIRC). The ITL's are company-sponsored technical specialty networks (e.g., ITLs on design automation, printers, or whatever). They send representatives from multiple locations to periodic, highly-technical internal conferences. They also provide other networking capabilities such as electronic conferencing. These are only a few examples of IBM's internal networking, sharing, and benchmarking.

In 1989, IBM Rochester also established an emphasis on external networking, sharing, and benchmarking. We sent representatives to 1988 Baldrige Award winners Motorola and Westinghouse Nuclear Fuels Division, to 1989 Baldrige Award winners Xerox and Milliken, to 1989 Deming Award winner Florida Power & Light, and to other world class companies like 3M, John Deere, Hewlett Packard, and Minneapolis Honeywell. Our representatives attended quality seminars and exchanged information about quality improvement ideas.

In addition, we invited some nationally recognized companies to send executives to visit IBM Rochester. These 1990 visitors included Xerox's CEO David Kearns, Motorola's Quality Vice President Paul Noakes and Director Ken Stork, Xerox book author and benchmarking expert Bob Camp, a small team of quality leadership managers from Xerox's Rochester, N.Y. facility, and Motorola's recently retired Quality Vice President Jack Germain.

Outbound and inbound visits were not the only way we learned and shared. Numerous telephone conversations were held with experts from the above-mentioned companies plus others (e.g., Corning, Unisys, and DEC). Note that sharing companies included IBM competitors (Hewlett Packard, DEC, Unisys, etc.), so we were careful to discuss only non-sensitive information dealing with personnel processes, facilities, education, and the like.

The net result was that IBM Rochester re-emphasized a broadened benchmarking in 1989 and in the following years. We did a lot of information collection, sharing, and benchmarking. There is a strong feeling that we are better for having done it.

Future Plans for Benchmarking

While IBM Rochester has recently made significant progress in improving the scope of its benchmarking, much remains to be done. Probably the biggest and most pressing need is to continue to improve benchmarking communication and sharing of information within IBM. The corporate benchmarking data base, the benchmarking Focal Point network, the conferences, and the electronic forum are all helpful. But they must all be strengthened, and our benchmarking people have to be taught to use them appropriately. Networking among benchmarking teams in different functions (e.g., manufacturing, hardware development, software development, personnel, etc.) needs to be initiated. As in so many facets of life, poor communications is at the root of many problems.

Also a consistent corporate-wide benchmarking management system is being developed. Currently, each benchmarking team is totally on its own regarding how it does benchmarking. Many helpful opportunities (e.g., classes, consulting, etc.) exist but none are required. The following management system requirements are under consideration:

- Should a benchmarking team be required to send at least one member to a benchmarking class (or read a benchmarking book) before it makes contact with a benchmarking partner group?
- Should the team likewise be required to check the corporate data base for pertinent past activity?
- Should the team be required to communicate with the IBM Sales Account Representative before contacting a partner company who is an IBM customer or even a potential customer?

All of these actions are currently encouraged but not required. The "Checklist" in Appendix C gives more possibilities. The question, of course, is how to promote efficient and effective benchmarking without making the process so bureaucratic that it discourages the teams from doing benchmarking. Several other benchmarking planned activities are also under development. They include:

- Improved benchmarking education.
- Improved benchmarking reporting.

- Merging the processes for IBM-initiated outgoing benchmarking and incoming benchmarking requests.
- Improvement of (and additions to) our internal benchmarking information sharing.
- Getting more management recognition for the fine efforts of Benchmarking Council representatives.

Lessons Learned from the Baldrige Application Process

An earlier section in this chapter discussed the 1989 Malcolm Baldrige National Quality Award (MBNQA) application process. Although IBM Rochester was a finalist and received a site visit by an MBNQA examiner team, we did not win an award in 1989. Note that we were not a loser; rather we were a non-winner. IBM did not lose by going through the application process. We gained immensely. Here were some of our conclusions:

- The 1989 award winners (Xerox and Milliken & Company) are world class and deserved to win this prestigious award.
- IBM Rochester scored well enough on our application to become a finalist.
- We are at (or very close to) world class in many of the award criteria.
- We produced a very worthwhile "wart list" for self-improvement.
- We gained experience in telling our story in a very concise application document and in hosting an examiner team for a site visit.

Benchmarking

- The examiner team feedback corroborated our wart list and found our application to be verifiable (maybe even a little conservative).
- We found that benchmarking is a significant contributor to the MBNQA scoring.

When we learned we were a 1989 Baldrige Award non-winner, there were only a few weeks to make a decision on whether to reapply in 1990. While disappointed by not winning, we learned some valuable lessons and started removing many of the warts. A decision was made to reapply in 1990. We did. And we won the award!

Here are some of the lessons learned from our experiences:

- The resources required to do a good self-evaluation and application are substantial, but the return on investment is even more substantial.
- The application information should be honest (an evaluator team visit will assure that it is) but not too modest or conservative, even if that is your nature.
- Get (and keep) top management involved in the process. In 1989, a top manager was assigned to lead in writing each of the seven criteria sections, but most of them soon went back to their regular work and only reviewed the work of the assigned staff. In 1990, a top manager was assigned to "own" each section and they remained deeply involved. Site General Manager Larry Osterwise owned Section 1 (Leadership) and was very active in its development.
- Appoint an organization-wide comprehensive application czar early in the application process. There are many

Chapter 5: What IBM Rochester Did to Facilitate Benchmarking

multi-section and cross-section considerations that require early and ongoing attention.

- Leave some time before the application deadline for trade-offs and polishing.

Applying for the Malcolm Baldrige National Quality Award (and its benchmarking implications) is a real experience. Try it—you'll like it (at least you will after its over).

SOME THOUGHT STARTERS!

1. How does (or would) benchmarking fit into your overall Total Quality Management system?

2. If your organization does not have top management support for benchmarking, how can that support be achieved? How can it be made clearly visible throughout the organization once it is achieved?

3. What mechanisms can best be used to share and communicate benchmarking plans and results in your organization?

4. How can truly effective benchmarking be stimulated and enabled?

5. How can you demonstrate that effective benchmarking does not require large resource allocations?

6/A Process for Effective Benchmarking

Introductory Comments

This chapter and the following five will describe a process for doing efficient and effective benchmarking (see Figure 8). Again, this author wishes to acknowledge and thank Bob Camp and the Xerox Corporation (as well as others with published processes) for their pioneer efforts. This process is similar to Camp's in many respects. It is modified and expanded to reflect the culture and situation within IBM. But all these published processes are philosophically very similar. The differences between this proposed process and the others are often small but very purposeful. This process has been taught to well over 700 IBM employees. They have

Benchmarking

Figure 8. The IBM Rochester Benchmarking Process

Subprocess	Steps		
I. Self-Introspection (Process Management)	1. Clarify your customers and outputs	2. Define appropriate benchmarking measurements	3. Review (and refine) your processes or product defns
II. Pre-Benchmarking (Preparation)	6. Set the level of data collection	5. Choose your benchmarking "partners"	4. Prioritize and select what is to be benchmarked
III. Benchmarking (Execution)	7. Collect data and organize it	8. Calculate gaps from your baseline	9. Estimate future attainable levels of achievement
IV. Post-Benchmarking (Project Management)	12. Implement actions and assure success	11. Set goals and action plans	10. Present benchmarking results
V. Review/Reset (Progress Assessment)	13. Review ongoing benchmarking integration	14. Assess progress toward goals	15. Reset goals and return to Step 1

helped to refine and tune it to fit IBM Rochester needs very well. This author believes it will fit the needs of most readers of this book.

First of all, the process is broken into five subprocesses, each of which contains three steps or tasks. Camp's process also had five sub-processes (not the same five however) containing 12 steps. His process looped back to Step 1 from Step 10, including four of the five subprocesses in the loop; this process includes all steps in the loop. There are several other subtle differences but the essence of this process and that used by Xerox and several other companies is the same. What is most important is that there be an organized process, and that it be carefully followed, to ensure success.

Clearly, any process containing five subprocesses and 15 steps can appear at first to be awesome and a resource gobbler. Several points need to be made to allay any such fears. Those points will be made in the remainder of this chapter.

Relationship to Process Management, Project Management, and Measurements

An initial point is that only seven of the 15 steps (less than half) are unique to benchmarking. Subprocesses II and III, and one step from Subprocess V are uniquely benchmarking. The other subprocesses should be part of quality management whether or not benchmarking is done. They are included in this benchmarking process description, because the benchmarking activity will be ineffective and inefficient without them. You cannot effectively compare yourself against others unless you thoroughly understand yourself first (i.e., Subprocess I—Process Management). You are wasting your time benchmarking (Subprocesses II and III) if you do not incorporate the findings into your future management actions (i.e., Subprocesses IV and V—Project Management and Progress Assessment).

The overlap of the benchmarking subprocesses and the basic requirements of sound management is a primary reason that benchmarking is not as formidable as it appears. However, it's also important to understand where the overlap ends—particularly in the area of process measurements.

Traditional process management tends to measure the way you are doing things today, with a lesser emphasis on customer service indicators. By contrast, benchmarking focuses much more heavily on external, customer-oriented measures. This point is discussed further in Chapter 7. Suffice it to say that use of traditional process measures in benchmarking would make it difficult to compare your performance to partner companies. Also, you would tend to discover ideas for incremental, business-as-usual improvements, rather than more valuable, breakthrough changes.

Three Additional Process Thoughts

Three more points need to be made about this benchmarking process. First, as was stated earlier, 15 process steps can seem rather awesome. Even the seven uniquely benchmarking steps can be seen as formidable. Several of the steps could consume considerable resources if benchmarkers allow themselves to become bogged down too long on any one step. Common sense must prevail. If a given step does not seem to apply to your particular situation, do it only to the extent that it benefits your activity (in rare cases, you may not do it at all). Each of these steps has a definite value-add in many situations, but some may not offer significant value-add to your specific case. In addition, do not allow yourself to get mired down in some of the more research-oriented steps (like selecting benchmarking partners).

Chapter 6: A Process for Effective Benchmarking

For these seemingly open-ended steps, use a couple of the suggested techniques that are cost-effective for you. When you have confidence that you have gone far enough, move on to the next step. For example, it is unnecessary to have selected the world's absolute best partner for what you wish to benchmark. What's important is that you have confidence that you have found a very good world class partner.

A second point is that this IBM Rochester Benchmarking Process seems to imply a very structured execution of this process with a loop back to Step 1 from Step 15. In practice, smaller internal loop-backs often occur. For example, this author has sometimes progressed to Step 7 (collecting the benchmark data) when discussions with a benchmarking partner brought to light a new benchmarking partner candidate that had not been discovered back in Step 5. If the new candidate had considerable merit, I would loop back to Step 5, include the new candidate, and apply Steps 6 and 7 to that organization before proceeding.

The third point is that Figure 8 implies a sequential step-by-step execution of the process. This ordering of these steps is intentional, but it is not sacred. In some cases, this author has reached Step 10 (communicate findings and get acceptance) and prepared to present recommendations to management. However, my style is to not present recommendations to management until I have at least a first-pass assessment of the cost of those recommendations. So I dip down to Step 11, estimate resources needed for some logical and possible action plan scenario, and incorporate it as a part of the Step 10 presentation. Again, let common sense guide the sequence of doing these tasks.

Simply stated, benchmarking (like so many other facets of real life) simply needs ample portions of common sense, flexibility, balance, and creativity to be successful. It is not free, but it is not overwhelming either. The ROI is almost always there when benchmarking is done effectively.

SOME THOUGHT STARTERS!

1. How would this benchmarking process fit into your organization's other quality and productivity improvement efforts?

2. What might be a scenario in which all 15 steps of this suggested benchmarking process were not necessary? Are there any steps that would never be useful in your organization?

3. How can we convince ourselves and others that a disciplined (but flexible) benchmarking process will lead to more effective benchmarking?

4. Should a process like the one proposed ever be used as evidence that an organization does not have enough available resources to do benchmarking? Why or why not?

7/Subprocess I—Self-Introspection (Process Management)

Introductory Comments

Subprocess I is a crucial prerequisite to benchmarking. Called self-introspection or process management, it is the subject of readily accessible classes and books. There are also several available computer tools to assist one in doing it. So it will not be covered in depth in this book.

Process management is a very common management tool which should be utilized periodically. As stated in the previous chapter, you cannot compare your own processes, products, services, etc., to others without first understanding yourself in some depth. Otherwise, you will probably waste your time, as well as the time of your benchmarking partners.

Some benchmarking authors regard process management as an implicit part of their process. This author found at IBM that all managers and process owners felt they had done it adequately. However, further questioning led to the discovery that in many cases it had been done only superficially or not for several years. Thus, process management is explicitly highlighted within this benchmarking process.

Other benchmarking authors make self-introspection activities explicit in their processes, but locate them within Step 7—Data Collection about themselves and about others. Again this author's experience is that there are advantages to doing it first. I believe that certain aspects of Steps 4 through 7 will be done more intelligently and effectively if self-introspection is done first. Often we cannot ask the right questions to collect the right data (in Step 7) unless we have previously given serious thought to our important measurements (Step 2). Yes, Subprocess I can be done concurrently with Steps 4-6 or within Step 7, but there are some advantages to doing it first if your schedule permits it.

This author recently heard a consultant making the case that Steps 1 and 2 are worthwhile, but Step 3 should be omitted. The consultant's premise was that to innovate and discover highly significant breakthrough improvements, one's mind is biased and preset by Step 3 to a point where one simply automates, simplifies, or refines the current process rather than recognizing an all new breakthrough method. While this author sees the danger pointed out by the consultant, I think it is more of a pitfall for internal brainstorming than for a process like benchmarking, which has an external focus.

Chapter 7: Subprocess I—Self-Introspection (Process Management)

STEP 1
Clarify Customers and Outputs

You must understand your outputs and customers in order to effectively prioritize and improve. Refer to Figure 9. The word "process" could be replaced by product, service, etc., and with slight modification, this discussion would apply just as well. In this figure, "your process" may be described as follows:

- If you are a manager, it may be all work under your direction (or an isolatable, significant piece of that work).

- If you are not manager but a team member, it may be the work of the entire team (or your part of it).

Figure 9. Transfer Function Chart

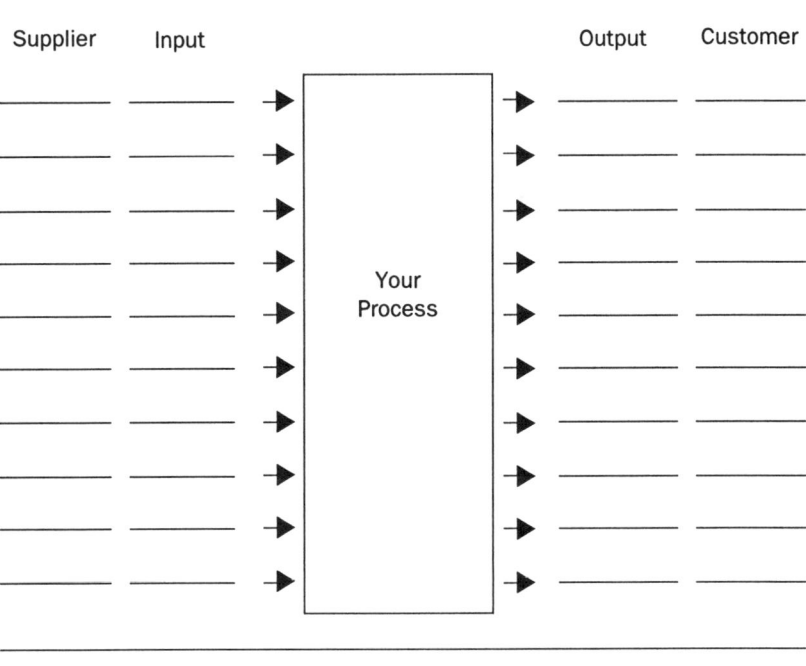

71

- It could be a cross-organizational process of which you are a part.
- Otherwise, it may be your current work assignment.

Your outputs are what you give to your customers. They are your reason for being on the payroll. The outputs of the entire workforce are the reason for your organization's existence. They are sometimes referred to as "deliverables" and are hopefully indicated in your group's mission statement. They are the product and result of your labors.

Your customers are those folks who receive your outputs. Earlier, this author made the point that your customers are frequently others working within your company or organization. They are those individuals or departments down the hall who are next in the "value-add" chain. Few people in business give their output directly to external customers. The point is to ensure that all your customers (internal or external) are satisfied—even delighted—with the output you give them. If all the internal customers along the chain are delighted customers, the probability of the external customer being delighted with the end product or service is greatly enhanced.

Clarifying outputs and customers is a valuable exercise. But don't let minute detail slow your activity. If you give a weekly status report (output) to your manager (customer), is that really significant to the benchmarking activity at hand? Probably not.

Don't forget (as Figure 9 reminds us) that most of you are customers too. Your suppliers give you input. If that input is unsatisfactory, you owe it to yourself to clarify requirements to those suppliers. If you have to fix a lot of errors in the input, you not only waste time, but sooner or later some of those defects will find their way into your output. Some suggestions are:

Chapter 7: Subprocess I—Self-Introspection (Process Management)

- Obtain customer review and comment on your outputs.
- Clarify your expectations to your suppliers.
- Prioritize your outputs.
- Use tools (like the transfer function chart in Figure 9) to document your process.
- Involve members of the benchmarking team early in the process of clarifying customers and outputs so that they see, hear, and understand as much as possible.

STEP 2
Define Appropriate Measurements

You must understand and choose important measurements of your outputs to effectively compare yourself against others. Those measurements should be general enough to be relevant to you and your benchmarking partner, yet specific enough to give useful results. The right set of measurements may be determined and prioritized by input from you, your team, your management and your customers. They should indicate how you measure success and quality. Even more importantly, they should indicate how your customers measure your success and quality.

Selecting good benchmarking measurements could start with your current measurement set. Review the measurements in your existing reports and in the pertinent literature. In some cases, there are widely-used standard measurements that can be used. Note that the benchmarking process may help you discover new useful measurements.

Your measurement set may contain indicators from generic areas like financial, technical, schedule, and performance or function. Hopefully, they also include measures of quality and customer satisfaction. If these last two categories are not covered, find meaningful metrics to cover them.

Sometimes your measurements must be combined with measurements of other related organizations. Since middle and senior managers are also "measured," your measurements may be combined with those from sister departments to form middle manager metrics. Those middle manager metrics may need to be combined with other related middle manager functions to form senior manager metrics. At any rate, your measurements should be meaningful and agreed upon.

The following is a key point. Not all meaningful and agreed-upon measurements are good benchmarking comparison measurements. Sometimes measurements are established for the purpose of controlling, monitoring, auditing, and improving your current process. Those measurements may be closely tied to the internal steps of your present process and may be necessary for internal management purposes. However, they are inappropriate for benchmarking comparisons. If the measurements are so integrally tied to how you do things now, it is unlikely that you will be able to use them to make comparisons with some other group that uses a very different (and possibly much better) internal process than you do.

So, the emphasis in setting good benchmarking measurements is for you to (mentally) step outside your process and look back at yourself as your customers see you. What are those quality, customer satisfaction, and performance measures that are important to your customers? Those customer perspective measurements tend to be good benchmarking comparison measures.

Proponents of re-engineering (a currently popular term which advocates throwing away all knowledge of the current process and starting over so that you do not end up with small, incremental, rather trivial improvements) would probably agree with this selection of measurements. They have a valid point. Benchmarking analysis must yield more than a few "tweaks" to a long-established process that really needs dramatic revamping.

So you may need to set aside many internal measures of your current process. You may also be tempted to set aside (from benchmarking comparisons) all measures that are considered to be "company confidential" or sensitive rather than entering into a formal non-disclosure agreement with other companies. But before these sensitive measures are set aside, consider whether they might be modified or converted to percentages, ratios, trends, etc., to remove their sensitivity yet preserve their value as a meaningful yardstick of comparison.

If after due consideration, benchmarking comparison metrics are still not forthcoming (or are very difficult or expensive to obtain), you may want to do a "mini-benchmarking activity" on finding a good measurement set. This may delay the primary benchmarking effort, but it could pay substantial dividends. This author's experience is that this interruption is rarely needed.

STEP 3
Review and Refine the Process Itself

This step is "standard fare" Process Management. If it has not been done recently in some detail (typically using some state-of-the-art analysis and documentation methods and tools), it should probably be redone. Things change. It is a rare manager or process owner who will admit that (s)he does not understand the details of the process, product, or service. So, even if a thorough understanding is claimed, it may be worthwhile to tactfully check.

The analysis should include flowcharting of subprocesses and individual steps or tasks. The boundaries of the flowchart should match the inputs and outputs of Figure 9 and the output measures from Steps 1 and 2. A natural fallout of this analysis is to watch for process simplification, cycle time reduction, and defect prevention improvements. Problems, issues, and challenges should be documented for further examination (possibly using a Pareto chart or fishbone diagram). Have the process flowcharts reviewed by implementation team members (and maybe some customers) to assure everyone sees things the way you do.

One difficult but worthwhile adjunct activity to Step 3 is to try to move your boundary of process analysis outward, so that it extends beyond your boundaries of responsibility. Understand what your customers do with your output after they receive it from you. Understand what your suppliers do to your input just before they give it to you. This may seem like extra work, but it can pay great dividends. The reason is simple. Your benchmarking partner may not have the same process boundaries as you do.

Often times process boundaries were set by organizational definition (department boundaries) or because they evolved that way over a number of years and for a number of reasons. Those reasons often do not include efficiency and effectiveness as primary goals. Process analysis looks at the internals of your process, but sometimes neither you nor your customers and suppliers analyze the boundary conditions.

This author's experience is that time and time again, changing those boundaries can have the greatest impact on elimination of hand-off defects and miscommunications, on removal of unwarranted delay times in transit, and on other shocking sources of quality degradation and customer dissatisfaction. My advice is scrutinize the process boundaries and handoffs, and watch closely those boundaries as you exchange information with benchmarking partners for better ideas.

SOME THOUGHT STARTERS!

1. Who are your customers and what are your outputs to them? Are your customers other people in your company or organization?

2. What are your key inputs and who supplies them to you? Are these suppliers also in your organization?

3. What measures of your suppliers' inputs are important to you? Do you think that those same measures are important to your customers' perspective of your outputs to them?

4. How long has it been since you really stepped back and analyzed your process for converting your inputs into your outputs? Is it time to do it again (or for the first time)?

5. Have you recently considered re-engineering your process (i.e., disregard entirely your current process and build a new optimal one from scratch)?

8/Subprocess II— Pre-Benchmarking (Preparation)

Introductory Comments

These three preparation steps are extremely important yet are frequently given superficial consideration by management and benchmarking teams. There seems to be a natural inclination by impatient benchmarkers to start shooting from the hip at this point—after all "we have decided to benchmark so let's go do it!" Or "I've got a brother-in-law in Company X, so let's call him and set up a visit!"

By rushing through the important "homework" involved in Subprocess II, the benchmarking activity effectiveness goes down. While there is less up-front investment, there is also usually considerably less value received. Short-changing Steps

4–6 turns the benchmarking activity into an "interesting visit" with marginal value.

While benchmarkers could meander around in this subprocess indefinitely, common sense says to do a few high-payback things and move on. Your challenge is to choose the right things to do.

STEP 4
Prioritize/Select What Is to Be Benchmarked

The point was made earlier that practically any process (or work output, product, or service) is a candidate for benchmarking. Your quality goal is to continuously improve so that everything you do becomes the best in the world. Since resources are finite, we must prioritize which things we want to benchmark fully now and which we want to defer (to some lower form of benchmarking or monitoring, or to internally-generated improvement recommendations).

The Self-Introspection Subprocess I assures that all processes (and needs) are analyzed, all have owners assigned, all products and services have been reviewed and so on. Now you must determine which have the highest priority for benchmarking due to low customer satisfaction, high defect rate, long cycle time, non-competitive performance, etc. The earlier discussion of measurements and gap analysis (remember Figure 5) will help. So will the decisions and emotions of top management. Certain unfortunate factors (resource constraints, politics, power struggles, etc.) sometimes become part of the prioritization, too. The key is to get the prioritization done and get on with it. Acknowledge your organization's culture and style, and use it to assure a good prioritization result.

Chapter 8: Subprocess II—Pre-Benchmarking (Preparation)

Also, part of Step 4 may be to finish Step 2 by prioritizing and selecting measurements which are appropriate to this benchmarking venture. As was stated, benchmarking measurements can "make or break" the activity so choose wisely. Remember the customer viewpoint throughout.

It is often helpful to ask yourself some key questions such as:

- What are your most important work products?
- Where is customer satisfaction the lowest?
- Where is competitive pressure the highest?
- How important is it to improve this target process?
- How applicable is benchmarking to this process?
- Did customer satisfaction viewpoint influence the process?
- Will improving the target process contribute to the company's strategy and plans?
- Will action taken as a result of benchmarking this process lead to more significant use of company resources than if you benchmarked other processes?
- If a questionnaire was developed from your measurements, would logical, usable data be obtained?
- Will these measures help you obtain useful data and information in a reasonably efficient and affordable manner?
- Can the data collected be used later to quantify the effect of implementing a new or modified process?

STEP 5
Choose Your Benchmarking Partners

More benchmarking teams seek out help on Step 5 than any other step. One reason is that all benchmarking teams must face this activity head on, while many other steps can be sidestepped or are easier or more natural. But again, Step 5 involves a lot of common sense mixed with some work. There are several things to consider.

First, set your benchmarking sights high. If you are going to spend resources doing significant comparisons against others, why not compare yourself to the very best you can find. Your goal is to become best so you have to deal with the best, and finding them may take a little creativity. However, your plans to compare yourself against the best may have to be tempered slightly by reality. When discussing types of benchmarking earlier, the author mentioned benchmarking with the best internal to your company or organization. These candidates are fairly easy to find and fairly easy to get data from (even sensitive data) but are unlikely to provide break-through ideas. It is this author's opinion that benchmarking against the internal best before going external is usually a good idea.

The other reality that may lower your sights from the world's best is the lack of resources. If that best company is in Japan or Europe, you may have to consider the North American best. Or sometimes a good benchmarking ROI can be achieved just benchmarking a very good but highly accessible organization. If there is a company with an excellent reputation (but not necessarily rated by you as best or even in the Top 5) and it is located just a few miles from you and is very willing to talk, this benchmarking-by-convenience may have a worthwhile ROI. Generally, you can learn something of value benchmarking many other organizations. But targeting comparisons with "the best" is going to usually make you best sooner.

The second thing to consider is that no company is best at everything it does. Just because some other group in your company or organization did their homework and determined Company X to be tops in their mutual field of interest does not necessarily mean that Company X is best at what you do. Just because a particular airline has an excellent measurement on safe landings does not mean that they are good at baggage handling or even at on-time arrivals. Just because a particular company has won a U.S. Malcolm Baldrige National Quality Award or a Japanese Deming Award, that does not mean that they are best at everything they do. They are probably very good at many things but not best at everything.

A third consideration is to avoid the temptation to take shortcuts and call Company X's vice president for quality because you read in the business press that they are the best. First, review the suggestions in this chapter and follow up on a few pertinent ones. The really good company names usually surface quickly, which will corroborate your hunches.

Another consideration is that much of the information you gather on the top companies at this point will be pertinent and helpful in later steps. Some of the benefits of an information search include:

- Catalogs existing information
- Helps define the options
- Focuses the investigation
- Establishes priorities for comparisons
- May develop leads to better sources of information
- Starts an ongoing, information-collecting process

- Makes a follow-up visit more efficient.

In addition, information gathered about a future benchmarking partner is useful as an icebreaker and rapport-builder if you end up visiting or calling them. A few compliments about recent accomplishments set a friendly tone and shows the partner that you cared enough to do some research. It also provides information about your partners sensitivities (like lawsuits or product failures) and helps you to avoid unintentionally embarrassing them. Much more about information gathering will be discussed later in this section.

Yet another Step 5 consideration is to try to keep it simple. For example, benchmarking with direct competitors (beyond traditional competitive analysis) can get complicated fast if your goal is a visit or phone conversation. You usually know who they are, but you are unlikely to discover breakthroughs. Meaningful information exchange is difficult unless you are discussing very general topics like personnel, facilities, education, etc. Even then, conversation is frequently very guarded and cautious to avoid losing any "competitive edge." Sometimes personal contact benchmarking with a direct competitor is worthwhile, but frequently it is not. It is always tense and cautious. Oftentimes you will find out more about a direct competitor from the public literature than from direct conversations.

Another aspect of keeping it simple is to seek out partners who have technical functions (or at least strong goals) similar to yours. Comparable functions are readily found within your industry, but do not define "industry" too narrowly. For example, IBM is in the computer industry but might well look to the electronics industry, the telecommunications industry, the office equipment industry, etc. Recall the discussion of functional benchmarking in Chapter 2, "Background."

Moving beyond Functional Benchmarking to Generic Benchmarking, you may seek to find meaningful comparisons of support functions (like personnel or finance) common to most industries. Or you may look for meaningful comparisons with dissimilar companies who have common goals to yours. This is probably best illustrated by the example in Bob Camp's book in which he and his Xerox colleagues benchmarked their warehousing and distribution functions against the L.L. Bean catalog distribution company. Clearly an efficient warehousing and distribution system is critical to the success of a catalog distribution company. L.L. Bean had implemented some methods which were significantly better than Xerox's and could even be termed breakthroughs.

Following this Generic Benchmarking line of thought (which Camp points out tends to improve the probability of a breakthrough idea), you should include in your benchmarking arsenal such thoughts as:

- If your objective is maximizing inventory turnover, consider organizations with perishable goods and/or low profit margins like the grocery store produce department or the florist.

- If your objective is fast customer service, consider organizations that survive on it like fast food companies.

- If your objective is ultra-high reliability, consider industries like aerospace or medical surgery.

- If your objective is minimizing high risk, consider industries like farming or high-risk insurance.

The remainder of this section is devoted to clues and suggestions for information sources and identification of best benchmarking partners. Much of this information is adapted from books by Robert Camp and by Leonard Fuld (see the bibliography for references) and the author is deeply grateful to them.

First, do the easy things—use internal information from your local (or company) experts and your local library. Then expand to other contacts and sources. Often the easy initial sources lead to other easy sources (by referral or bibliography). This author has found these initial sources to be tremendously helpful with very little personal time investment. More ideas are found in Step 6 (Set a Level of Data Collection).

To identify the best benchmarking partners, consider the following information sources (many of which can be found by talking to the right people or visiting a library):

- Subject matter experts in your company/organization
- Other departments/sites within your business
- Other companies within your industry
- Direct product competitors
- Leadership companies/functions
- World class process experts
- Annual reports and 10K data
- Industry periodicals with "top 100 companies . . . " analyses
- Published data, industry averages, studies, surveys
- Research librarians
    - Public data bases (rapid and inexpensive)
    - Professional and trade associations (industry or discipline specific)
- Consultants

- Electronic data base services
- Vendors/customers

Camp's book breaks information sources into internal (to your company or organization), external, and research. Some novel internal sources could include reviews of products or services, or some publications not distributed externally. Some external information sources might include conferences and seminars, product expositions, professional society and industry publications, newsletters, and the like. Sources of information in the research category would include such examples as consultant reports, surveys and questionnaires, or networks.

Some other sources:

Questionnaires/Surveys	Government Documents
Magazine/Journal Articles	State Corporate Filings
Data Bases	Conference Proceedings
Special Magazine Issues	State Industry Directories
Wall Street Transcript	Foreign Sources
Current Industrial Reports	Credit Services
Management Biographies	Industry Listings
Financial Periodicals	Statistical Sources
Buyers Guides	Investment Manuals
Recent Books	Verbal Referrals
Published Reports	R&D Sources
Trade Shows	Environmental Impact Reports

STEP 6
Set a Level of Data Collection

It was established earlier that benchmarking could employ part or all of a hierarchy of data collection levels. This section will explore some examples of those various levels and some overall considerations and suggestions.

First, data collection on world class companies as potential benchmarking partners should be an ongoing process, not a short-term event. This author contends that many organizations do ongoing benchmarking (industry monitoring, competitive analysis, quality improvement idea seeking, etc.) without even thinking of it as benchmarking. You are doing what I call "low-key benchmarking" when you:

- Read professional society journals
- Attend conferences and product expositions
- Read the business newspapers and periodicals
- Watch a story about a competitor on the TV news

These are basic bottom-of-the-hierarchy activities. You can use these methods for those processes, products, and services which you prioritized low to medium in Step 4. In addition, since benchmarking is defined as a continuous and iterative process with a loop back from the last to the first step, the next loop through the process is made much easier by continual low-level monitoring.

Camp and many other sources describe some characteristics of data that you might choose to collect. A brief consideration of these characteristics can lead the benchmarker to more efficient data collection. Some of these characteristics are:

- Type of data (single point, trend, ratio, etc.)
- Amount of data (time available to collect, verification needed, etc.)
- Accuracy of data (precision, verification, importance, etc.)
- Cost of data (dollars, time to collect/analyze, etc.)
- Collector of data (self, colleagues, consultants, librarians, etc.)

Clearly, some of these characteristics are determined or influenced by the decisions you made back in Steps 2 and 4 on your benchmarking measurement set.

The data collection methods used by the benchmarking team will certainly effect the cost and value of the data gathered. A brief listing (with inexpensive but general data at the top and more expensive but more valuable data proceeding downward) follows:

- Literature Review
    - Internal to your company/organization
    - External
- Research Reports
    - Surveys
    - Consultant Studies
- Direct Contact
    - Correspondence
    - Telephone or video conferences
    - Site visits

Figure 10 illustrates a benchmarking data collection hierarchy with the inexpensive general data at its base.

Common sense tells benchmarkers to use the data collection methods that are easy and inexpensive first, then proceed up the Figure 10 hierarchy until you have reached a comfort level that allows you to proceed to Step 7. This author has usually found it worthwhile to use a combination of methods selected from several hierarchy levels. The following are recommended:

- Literature Search—Always do some; focuses direction

Benchmarking

Figure 10. A Benchmarking Data Collection Hierarchy

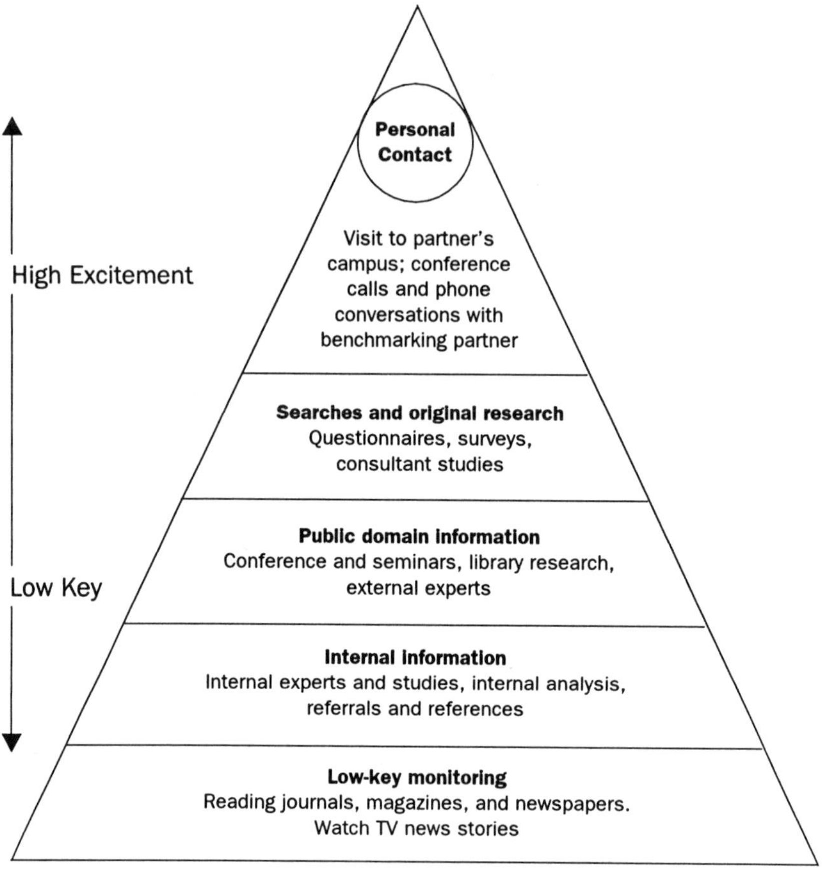

- Talk to Experts—Almost always do some, especially in-house experts
- Research—Do if needed; expensive and takes longer
- Contact Partner—Do if affordable; faster and riskier but higher potential

There is somewhat of a logical progression in data collection. It usually goes as follows:

- Use low-key monitoring continuously
- Then seek internal information
- Proceed to external public domain information
- Conduct searches and original investigations as needed
- Make personal contact with the best

Internal information tends to be highly accessible. Seeking it out is usually very productive and inexpensive (in your time and budget). Appreciation goes to Camp for much of the following thoughts on seeking internal information:

- Product analysis
  - Your products
  - Competitors' products
- Company sources
  - Internal organizations
  - Gather documented data
  - Functional experts
  - Operational managers
  - Leads to referrals/references/sources
  - Also alerts others that you are seeking the data
- Data from existing/proposed studies
  - Existing studies often broad enough to be helpful
  - Proposed studies might dovetail with your research
  - Use electronic networks (or meetings)

- Internal experts and studies
  - Corporate/industry awareness groups
  - Business-wide consultant studies
  - Corporate data bases

Public domain information is the next logical step. It is very accessible and seeking it out is usually productive. However, it takes a little more work and resources. Here are some thoughts about this type of information:

- Library research (librarian can watch for information of interest)
  - Periodicals, annual reports, etc
  - Professional society journals
  - Documents in public electronic data bases
  - Seminar talks
  - Conference proceedings
  - Newspaper articles
  - Government reports
- Attend seminars, conferences, trade shows, association meetings
  - Talks
  - Displays
  - Tours
  - Brochures, handouts
- Consultants
  - Serve as intermediaries with well-designed questions

- Conduct surveys, searches
- Do analyses
- Critique your findings
- Provide anonymity, non-bias, validation
- Consultant selection is important
* External experts and studies
  - Brokerage firms
  - Financial institutions
  - Universities
  - Non-profit organizations
  - "Watchdog" organizations
  - Consumer advocate groups
  - Retirees

Original research and investigations can certainly be of great benefit under certain circumstances. But it tends to be expensive and time consuming, so this author recommends judicious use (usually to improve data accuracy and completeness or to fill gaps in information collected from other sources). Here are some additional thoughts:

* Questionnaires/surveys
  - Questions are documented and consistent
  - Permits more extensive data gathering
  - Can ensure anonymity and confidentiality
  - May need face-to-face between third-party and respondee to clarify/assist

- Different completion methods
    - Mail
    - Telephone
    - Filled out by visiting third party
    - Filled out by visiting benchmarking team
- Filters/dilutes information
- No direct site observations/contacts
- Useful for clear-cut question situations
- Different types
    - Multiple choice
    - Forced choice
    - Open ended
    - Scaled
- Questions can be derived from cause-and-effect diagrams of the process
- Easy questions first, hard ones later
- Be selective and focused in data you request

The following are a few concluding thoughts about Step 6—"Set a Level of Data Collection":

First, back in Step 1 there was mention of the need to pick the benchmarking team early. If that has not been completed yet, Step 6 is the stage of the process to do it. This author, when teaching benchmarking to IBM employees, refers to the "home team" and to a possible "traveling squad." The home team can be one to several (possibly a dozen) people

Chapter 8: Subprocess II—Pre-Benchmarking (Preparation)

with certain talents and expertise. Some characteristics that this home team should possess are:

- Technical knowledge to understand answers to benchmarking questions/measures, and to answer questions from benchmarking partner regarding your operation.
- Knowledgeable managers in whose areas changes would have to be implemented.
- Expertise in the benchmarking process itself.
- Possibly a customer to add the customer viewpoint to benchmarking interchange.
- Skills to deal with consultants or company representatives.
- Interpersonal skills. The success of an ongoing benchmarking partnership often depends on a successful first impression.

The traveling squad is a subset of the home team and is called upon if an actual site visit is made (or possibly if a limited attendance conference call or video conference is arranged). This group should be small (typically one to three members) and should contain the following talents/expertise (in priority order):

1. In-depth subject matter expertise of the benchmarked process, product, or service. Hopefully, the traveling squad will include a respected member of the implementation team so that (s)he can help produce the team "buy-in" and "feeling of ownership" when improvement changes are recommended.

2. Authority to change benchmarked processes. Hopefully, the traveling squad will include a manager in the area

where improvement changes will likely result. This person will also be a powerful benchmarking team ally later in the process.

3. Someone (if not the persons described above) with a perspective broader than the specific process, product, or service being benchmarked. Recall the earlier discussion of the value of comparing the boundaries of your process with those of your partners. This person provides this comparison, and possibly some broader view of the business/organization itself.

So the "traveling squad" needs considerable expertise and knowledge. But resources sometimes limit the squad to one or two. Your challenge is to pick the person(s) best suited to ask the right questions, understand the answers, and respond to your benchmarking partners' questions.

One final point is to again urge that the benchmarking team not "gloss over" or skimp on the Subprocess II preparation steps. Experience proves that a little up-front investment pays big dividends later.

Chapter 8: Subprocess II—Pre-Benchmarking (Preparation)

SOME THOUGHT STARTERS!

1. Who in your organization should determine the priorities of what should be benchmarked? Who should provide input to help those decision makers?

2. Do the same decision makers determine what metrics are most meaningful in the benchmarking activity? Why or why not?

3. Are benchmarking partners chosen out of convenience? From companies about which you have heard good things? Where you have contacts already? From sound research? All of the above?

4. Can worthwhile benchmarking be done without actually making a site visit?

9/Subprocess III—Benchmarking (Execution)

Introductory Comments

You have finally reached the heart of the benchmarking. The preparation done, it is now time for the core work—and the payback for our efforts. In Subprocess III, you collect benchmark data, compare it to your baseline analysis, and analyze what it will take for your organization to become the best.

STEP 7
Collect the Data and Organize It

Step 6 concentrated on levels of data collection and typical sources. The next step may bring you to the peak of the

Benchmarking

Figure 10, a site visit to a benchmarking partner. Step 7 also encompasses general data collection and organization.

First of all, some of the data collected in Step 5 (choose partners) will contribute to the overall data collection of this step. Some of Step 5 information pertained to key measures of how good the potential partners really are. Your task now is to gather any needed information about the chosen partner organization so that you can compare its achievement level to yours (using your key measurements from Step 2). Then you can analyze the performance gaps and reasons for those gaps.

Finding the needed information is the heart of the whole benchmarking process. Solid credible data will be needed to convince top management to implement changes to close the performance gaps. To do a "quickie" or "cheapie" shortcut job at this step is cheating yourself and your organization.

Data collection is not always easy and straightforward. But it should always be ethical and above board. Espionage or other unethical procurement of information should never be even considered. Good data collection may require:

- Inquisitiveness
- Persistence
- Resourcefulness
- Assertiveness
- Ingenuity
- Common Sense

There are two key considerations in collecting data. First, data is needed not only about achievement levels but also (whenever practical) about methods and practices used to achieve those admirable levels of performance. Second, you should be prepared to reciprocate with comparable information about your organization. Benchmarking is a two-way, mutually beneficial exchange.

So the actual data collection goes as high on the Figure 10 hierarchy as is needed and justified by your resources and priorities. Clearly, in many benchmarking activities sufficient data is available even if you stay in the lower four levels (low-key monitoring, internal information gathering, public domain information gathering, and searches and original research). Thus, no reciprocation and information sharing is necessary.

But probably the most exciting and often most rewarding data collection is the top hierarchy level (direct personal contact). Even at this level, there are several sublevels. These start with exchanging written information, move up through telephone contacts, video conference meetings, and culminate with site visits. Through all four of these sublevels, this author strongly recommends that you take time to prepare a set of key questions before the contact. That list of questions should reflect your key measurements and your desire to know how the partner achieves benchmark levels of performance. The list should not be too cumbersome or time-consuming for your partner. It should be prioritized with top-priority questions first. Also, preparing a list of questions focuses your thoughts so that you effectively utilize the partner's time. It also helps you to clarify any potential concerns about confidentiality of information you're seeking. Remember, never ask your benchmarking partner for information that you would be unwilling to share about yourself. If the partner contact is in writing only (possibly preceded by an introductory brief phone call), the list of questions could take the form of a formal questionnaire. But usually the less formal, the better.

If the contact is by phone, video conference, or visit, the question list serves as a checklist or outline for discussion.

However, one must be knowledgeable and flexible in order to follow-up on unclear or surprising answers.

It is usually advantageous to send the list of questions to your benchmarking partner before your call, video conference, or visit. That gives your partner host:

- Time to think about answers
- Time to gather data needed
- Time to evaluate confidentiality of intended answers
- Time to get the right people to the call or meeting

In making contact with a benchmarking partner, there are a few hints (again common sense) to keep in mind. A bad initial contact can lead to a turn down or a poor relationship. A useful guideline is to treat your first contact with a benchmarking partner as though it were the start of a long-time, ongoing friendly relationship. Then you are in the right frame of mind. Here are some other thoughts:

- Be concise about the purpose and objectives of the contact.
- Be yourself (open, honest, friendly).
- Compliment the partner about something they have done well lately (based on information gathered in Step 5)
- Share something interesting/useful about your organization.
- Know of any customer or supplier relationships between the partner and you (if they are a customer, let your sales account representative know about your contact; if they are a supplier, notify your purchasing representative).
- Mail or fax a benchmarking proposal that can be discussed by interested parties in their organization.

The site visit to a benchmarking partner's campus is usually the most interesting, exciting, and credible method of data collection. The following are some components of and guidelines for a direct site visit:

- Face-to-face exchange of data/information.
- Often coupled with a tour.
- Observations, nonverbal communication, casual comments are informative.
- Spontaneous, unscripted exchanges.
- May lead to unexpected ideas. May also cause tension over issues of confidentiality.
- Use short on-site time to the maximum.
    - Making contact to set up the visit
    - Determining who should attend
    - Developing the itinerary/agenda
    - Conducting the actual visit
    - Debriefing/documenting after the visit
- Careful planning and preparation are essential to ensure productive use of each party's time.
- Do your homework on public information about your partner before the visit.
    - Annual reports.
    - Dun & Bradstreet report.
    - Recent articles in journals, newspapers.
    - Recent ad campaigns.

- Do not bring up negative information to agitate.
- Compliment and show knowledge while setting up the visit.

If a site visit is planned, it is often beneficial to get agreement in advance on the visit agenda. Here are some considerations for a benchmarking agenda:

- Get agenda agreement early in contact negotiations.
- Send confirmatory letter, agenda, and set of discussion questions to partner in advance.
  - Confirms intentions
  - Gets right people to meetings
  - Allows hosts to think about questions
- Start visit with introductions and two-way process overviews.
- Represent yourself honestly and be open with your contacts.
- A tour is often beneficial.
- Take notes with some discretion (e.g., don't try to write down everything they say).
- Side discussions or wrap-up can confirm understanding.
- Use informal times (breaks, lunch, tours, etc.) to build rapport and gain additional information.
- Seek expert opinions on problems and highlights.
- Ask about non-confidential plans.
- Be prepared to explain why you are asking any question.
- Decide what information about your organization you are willing to leave behind.

- If appropriate, offer a reciprocal visit to your site.
- Take notes on promises made, then follow through.
- Thank the host(s).

On a site visit, be sure to send the right team. It will be laying the foundation for what could be a long-term relationship. Here are some characteristics of an optimal team:

- Professionals, managers, company reps, third parties (such as consultants).
- Must be knowledgeable about the process/company.
- Must be congenial.
- Do not send a plane load and overwhelm the host.
- Do not send people with potentially conflicting or distracting agendas (sales, contracting, etc).
- A visiting team of one to three members (for a given process) is ideal, according to Robert Camp, with the team members sharing and rotating duties like asking questions and recording answers.
- Team should/could include:
  - Subject matter expert
  - Person responsible for benchmarking
  - Person responsible for implementing changes
  - Person from site/HQ planning/analysis
- Team should discuss plan before the visit.
- Team should have a lead person.
- Team should not be critical of host's process.
- Concentrate on what the host does better.

Benchmarking

After a site visit there is still lots of work to do. Here are some thoughts about that:

- Send a letter (or phone call) of appreciation promptly.
- Debrief the session.
  - ASAP after meetings (on site, at airport, at your nearby branch office)
  - Confirm/augment notes and "to do's"
  - Cross-check facts and observations
  - Determine value/priority of new information
- Prepare a trip report.
  - Summarize key findings
  - Use follow-up telephone calls to clear confusions
  - Attach useful/needed data
  - Copy appropriate persons outside the visit team
  - Send copy to benchmarking partner host if appropriate

Remember, if a site visit is not well prepared and well conducted, it turns effective benchmarking into an interesting visit.

Before leaving the subject of contacts with benchmarking partners, Camp (and others) suggest an alternative to a one-on-one contact. Camp calls it a "Benchmarking Focus Group." It is a mini-conference in which several benchmarking partners can share information in a small group setting. While this author has not yet used this technique, he can envision scenarios where it could work very well. It is included here as yet another consideration for the reader.

- Technique uses sharing by benchmarking focus groups.

- Could use third party to:
  - Make arrangements
  - Act as facilitator
- Setting could be a panel discussion.
  - Agreed-upon topics
  - Neutral site or host site
- A variation is a "panel discussion in writing" (a delphi)
  - Panelists respond in writing to a list of questions.
  - Responses are merged and sent back to panelists to stimulate further thought.
  - Process continues for several cycles.
- Document results to participants

STEP 8
Calculate Gaps to Baseline

Benchmarking gaps are simply differences in important measures between your performance and where you would like to be. Recall the spider chart of Figure 5 that helped benchmarkers to visualize some gaps. Now you are armed with information to plot actual gaps, not just perceived gaps on the spider chart.

The first key is to assure that the benchmarking activity does not die away after the visit to a partner's location (or other forms of data collection). Unless some exciting breakthrough has been discovered, there might be a tendency to doze off and regress to business as usual. If you are to get an ROI from benchmarking, the remainder of the benchmarking process must be completed. Allocation of future resources can depend on this activity.

Benchmarking

A second post-data-collection analysis is useful to briefly review your measurement set (from Step 2) and see if benchmarking has taught you some better ways of measurement. If so, you may want to temporarily slip back to Subprocess I and see if you can gather input about yourself so that the newly discovered metrics can be included in your gap analysis.

Baseline data has been gathered in Steps 1–3. You have gathered benchmark data in Steps 4–7. Gap analysis is simply investigating the differences.

Benchmarking gaps come in three flavors: good gaps, small gaps, and bad gaps (Camp calls them positive, parity, and negative gaps).

"Good gaps" occur when your own achievement levels are greater than those of your benchmarking partner. You are ahead (or best). If you have done a good job back in Step 5 of choosing best benchmarking partners and if you have done an accurate job of collecting measurement data, good gaps do not happen very often. Cherish them! But remember Figure 1. If an organization becomes complacent, it will not have a good gap very long. Outperforming benchmarking partners does not mean that you should stop improving those processes, products, or services (especially if the gap is small and/or if there is a large gap from baseline to total customer satisfaction). It is not a waste of resources to widen a good gap. It could also be a clue as to what to stress in your next ad campaign. It may be an indicator that the processes implementation group deserves rewards or recognition. The bottom line is that even a sizeable good gap—if your improvement rate is slow—is in danger of being surpassed by a hard-charging competitor.

"Small gaps" imply that you are in the same ball park as your benchmarking partner. It is nice to think that you are among the best but the same warnings apply here (even more so) as for good gaps. Being comparable to the best is not a license to relax. Use the data you have gathered from your partners on how they achieve their performance levels. It is this author's experience that sometimes a small gap can be changed to a good gap by using some of that information.

"Bad gaps" are the normal results of good benchmarking. They indicate that your performance lags behind the best. This is a call to action that promotes the need for a strong improvement plan. Improvement changes can narrow bad gaps, and can also improve image, raise internal morale, and provide other intangible benefits.

Remember, gap analysis does not always involve quantitative (numeric) measurement data. Sometimes the data is qualitative (descriptive). Both have value and both can be used in comparisons. Note the CIM maturity index gap analysis described in Chapter 13, "An IBM Rochester Gap Analysis Example." Qualitative data may be mapped (or converted somehow) onto relative scales, or the gap analysis may be based on "gut feelings." Either way, it has value and can lead to significant improvement.

Finally, analytic gap analysis is only one form of judging superiority in the eyes of customers. Customer perceptions are not always captured in our analyses. Customer requirements are not always synonymous with customer desires. Do not let benchmarking analysis take you away from what gives you a competitive edge—awareness of the customer viewpoint.

STEP 9
Estimate Future Achievement

This is the step where you set the change points illustrated in Figure 4—shooting at a flying duck. The benchmarking team must now make some key decisions on what they want to recommend. What will it take for you to be the best in a reasonable time frame with an acceptable investment?

The team may want to start by calling in extra expertise. They may want to reaffirm their understanding of (and confidence in) the benchmarking gap analysis. They may want to review all they learned from benchmarking partners about how the world class achievement levels were accomplished. They will hopefully incorporate good improvement ideas from the organization's own employees. Any "breakthrough" ideas should surface quickly.

Then some charting should start. Figure 11 is an example of how the benchmarking team could start estimating their projections of future achievement of both their own organization (under a set of improvement assumptions) and of the benchmarking partner. The improvement line shown by Numbers 1 (historical performance), 2 (current baseline), and 3 (business-as-usual improvement) are the current plan. Note that Point 3 does not indicate a do-nothing plan of improvement, but rather a continued improvement at the same rate as in the recent past.

The improvement line projected for the benchmarking partner is shown by Numbers 4 (current benchmark achievement level) and 5 (projected future improvement slope). It is natural to ask, How does the team ever project the future performance of a different organization? The following are some sources of guidance:

- Information from literature search (Steps 5 and 6)
- Information from the contact or visit (Step 6)
- Partner's historical trends
- Industry trends
- Data extrapolations

Chapter 9: Subprocess III—Benchmarking Execution

Figure 11. A Gap Analysis Chart

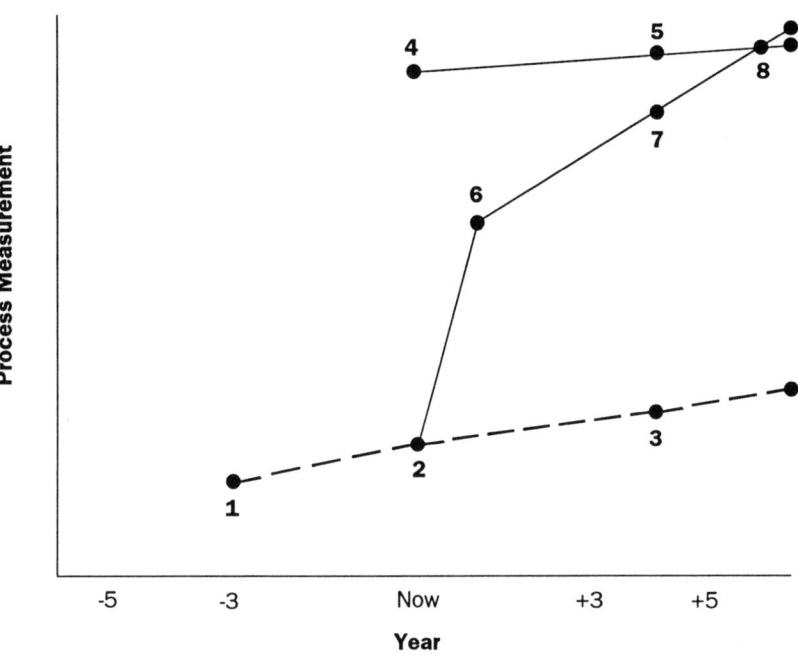

1. Our measurement history
2. Our current process measurement (baseline)
3. "Business as usual" improvement
4. Current benchmark level
5. Projected benchmark improvement
6. One-time incremental change improvement (tactical)
7. Projected new process improvements (strategic)
8. Intersection point with partner

- Gut feelings

Note that in Figure 11, Line 1-2-3 and Line 4-5 are converging. Theoretically, at some point in the future, the organization might catch its benchmarking partner. If these lines are diverging, your present course will soon put you out of business.

Of course, the benchmarking team didn't complete the previous steps just to learn that someday they might catch up. Now the team needs to examine some scenarios for change that would accelerate their organization's rate of improvement. They also need to make sure that improving the benchmarked process will not undermine other processes.

Figure 11 shows that rapid deployment of one or more changes could cause a short-term dramatic improvement to Point 6. Other improvements might result in a steeper improvement slope to Point 7. At the Point 8, the slope intersects with the benchmarking partner's line. In about 5.5 years, the organization has become the best.

A family of such curves (defined by Points 2-6-7-8) should be developed and analyzed according to cost, risk and schedule. Armed with these analyses, the team is prepared to make and justify a recommendation.

Chapter 9: Subprocess III—Benchmarking Execution

SOME THOUGHT STARTERS!

1. Is any of the data collected in Step 5 "Choose Your Benchmarking Partner" of value at this stage? If yes, for what purpose? If no, did you carry Step 5 far enough?

2. If a site visit is a part of your data collection, what should you do before and after the visit to make it as effective as possible?

3. How will you share information? With whom? Why? What is in it for you?

4. What is the most effective way for you to present your gap analysis to the "change agents" in your organization?

5. What innovative (but ethical) methods can be used to predict future performance achievements of benchmarking partners and competitors?

10/Subprocess IV—Post-Benchmarking (Project Management)

Introductory Comments

The activity unique to benchmarking is now finished, except for a short review in Step 13. Now the process returns to the things you need to do whether or not you are benchmarking. This is conventional project management (sometimes called change management) in which improvement changes are considered and implemented. Hopefully, the benchmarking activities of Steps 4 through 9 will enable you to make better and bigger improvements than without them. In this age when your competitors continue to improve, for you to stand still is tantamount to losing ground.

This post-benchmarking subprocess is critical to the successful use and implementation of what you have learned.

Without it, the preceding nine steps of the process were simply academic exercises with no ROI. You must continue through the process to make things happen.

STEP 10
Present Benchmarking Results

All can be lost if results are presented poorly. Doing a good "staff job" consists of assembling credible, clear, and convincing arguments, then using effective presentation techniques. You will often be competing for resources and recommending unnatural changes. If the effects of benchmarking are not accepted, your organization will likely revert to business-as-usual project management.

You must always remember that human nature includes a natural reluctance to change, especially if that proposed change affects one's own job. Reaction to change recommendations ranges from outright hostility or skepticism to acceptance or occasional enthusiasm. (Some early discussion of preliminary findings will help reduce management's resistance to change.)

The purpose of this step is to encourage enthusiasm (or at least acceptance) even if your organization is doing "pretty good" and is not in a crisis situation. The purpose of benchmarking is to set challenging goals in order to promote improvement and change beyond "business as usual." Sometimes strategic redirection is involved. Therefore, to be successful, you must gain understanding and acceptance by two key audiences. One audience is the management decision-making team that controls resource allocation and change implementation. The other audience is those employees "in the trenches" who will be affected.

There are three essential steps to gaining understanding and acceptance by these two key audiences.

Chapter 10: Subprocess IV—Post-Benchmarking (Project Management)

- Study the audience and its needs
- Tailor the communications to the audience
- Organize the communication for overall understanding

Different forms of communication work best for different circumstances and different audiences. Some of the forms are:

- Written (status report, trip report, newsletter, etc.).
- Electronic (requests, networking report)
- Oral (in-person presentation)

This author usually prefers oral presentation when the opportunity presents itself. You gain the benefits of non-verbal communication, group interaction, and real time answering of questions. However, the success of oral presentations hinges on effective speaking techniques.

Communication on a benchmarking analysis is usually organized with key elements. These include:

- A summary of findings and recommendations.
- Description of the study process and analysis.
- More detail on findings and conclusions.
- Attached backup information.

Maximizing acceptance by the audience involves several techniques, including:

- Use meaningful interesting graphics
- List the benefits
- Bridge to today's strategy and plan
- Explain changes and operational impact

- Cite precedents and benchmarks of world class organizations
- Validate from multiple sources if possible

The purpose of communication is to gain the support, ownership, and commitment of all levels of the audience. This acceptance may be demonstrated in a number of ways:

- Position of involved senior leadership
- Written responses
- Requests for additional change implementation information
- Tone of meetings
- Questions and nonverbals
- Consensus

Some overall recommendations include:

- Be sure to tune the communication to the audience(s).
- Target persuasion to key (especially hostile) people.
- Anticipate questions/concerns and be prepared to address them.
- If there is a particularly concerned group, consider a special preview presentation directly to them to minimize and neutralize their concerns.
- Use graphic gap information.
- Be prepared to address how things might look after (and if) the proposed changes aren't implemented.
- Ask for agreement to proceed (if appropriate).

Chapter 10: Subprocess IV—Post-Benchmarking (Project Management)

During Step 10, it is understandable to want to involve the implementation team as soon as is practical. Their suggestions and improvements can improve the overall proposal. Their buy-in and feeling of ownership are crucial to a later successful implementation. But consideration must be given to involving this team too deeply too soon. If the management team has not been made aware of the proposal and has not given at least a preliminary okay, they may be unpleasantly surprised to learn of the implementation team's involvement. On the other hand, the implementation team usually has a very good network and is very aware that benchmarking is going on and changes are being considered. If they do not know what is being proposed until after full management approval, they may feel left out and that the changes are being crammed down their throats. They feel no ownership and may impede successful implementation.

So, the benchmarking team walks a fine line in bringing both audiences along appropriately. The process is affected by the organization's culture regarding participative management. Appropriate selection of benchmarking team members can alleviate this dilemma. The technical subject matter expert represents the implementation team and an affected manager represents the management team.

STEP 11
Set Goals and Action Plans

This step emphasizes conventional project management. As in the case of Subprocess I (Process Management), there are many readily accessible books and classes on setting goals and action plans. So only a few highlights will be given here.

First, this step involves both long-term and short-term goal setting. Long term is usually called "strategic" and short term is frequently called "tactical" or "operational." Thus, there is a goal setting hierarchy which may be described as follows:

- Overall mission (rarely changes)
- Planning principles (occasionally change)
- Strategies (regularly updated)
- Performance goals (frequently change)
- Tactics (frequently updated)
- Operating plan goals (regularly and frequently change)

This goal setting hierarchy shows that the organization can and will make improvement changes to better meet customer needs and achieve best levels of performance.

Benchmark data is a statement of best practices while goals are a statement of planned performance. Therefore, your task in this step is to convert benchmark (and other) findings into a statement of operational goals. This can be done by creating operating (planning) principles from benchmark conclusions. These operating principles can be a clear statement of change which describes:

- What will be incorporated into new goals
- How the organization will change over time
- How the organization will look after the changes are fully implemented

Good goals are very challenging, yet realistic and attainable. While they should not force doing "too much too soon," which creates frustration and a sense of failure, the longer term goals should clearly be "very difficult" to force organizations out of their incremental business-as-usual improvement mentality. Some highly successful quality improvement program participants have commented that in retrospect their goals (which were often viewed by implementation teams as unattainable) were too timid. They did not stretch far enough to "shoot ahead of the flying duck."

Then good goals should be transformed into good plans. What are you going to do now (or soon) to achieve the goals? Plans involve resource allocation and schedule setting. These plans may range from a very resource-constrained attempt to reach full entitlement to a "whatever it takes" plan for rapid goal achievement. While the goal setting may be strongly influenced by the management team, the plan determination should deeply involve the implementation team. If significant change is planned, training and education (and other enablers) of the team should be included in the plan.

Finally, the plans should include continued appropriate benchmarking. The goals are to close the benchmarking "bad gaps," and those gaps have two endpoints—baseline and benchmark. Ongoing monitoring of your organization yields updated baseline. Ongoing benchmarking yields updated benchmarks.

STEP 12
Implement Actions and Assure Success

This step is just plain good management. The action plans must clearly show schedules and allocated resources as well as the expected result. Some strategic or temporary redirection of resources may be needed. Education and training (or retraining) for affected employees and their managers must be available if and when needed. Change leadership must remember that normal change is cause for apprehension, but dramatic change can be downright scary.

The implementation team should be aware not only of

their own measurement goals but also of those for the company or larger organization. Team members can then understand how they fit into the big picture. Standard straight forward changes are usually implemented by line management or a dedicated functional team. Work process related practice changes may be better implemented by a performance team (or quality circle) responsible for its operation.

If the changes are broad, multifunctional, or even multisite, they should be managed accordingly. The possibility of a senior management project "czar" may be a consideration. For a multisite or multi-group change, an early pilot implementation may be advantageous. The pilot group or site should be carefully picked to provide:

- An enthusiastic and committed implementation team
- A straightforward, uncomplicated application
- A dramatic improvement potential
- A high probability of early success

This result then can be used as a role model for implementation at other sites or groups.

Traditional project management techniques apply. Keep the project on schedule and at planned cost. Detect problems early (anticipate them if possible) and resolve them quickly. Management should be interested and involved, but the implementation team needs room to operate.

Chapter 10: Subprocess IV—Post-Benchmarking (Project Management)

SOME THOUGHT STARTERS!

1. How can you analyze your audience before presenting your benchmarking results? How can you neutralize any antagonist's arguments?

2. What is the best way for you to use benchmarking results in goal setting? In formulating and implementing action plans?

3. What other actions can help assure success of approved planned changes in your organization?

4. What resistance might you expect, and from whom? What can you do to counteract it?

11 / Subprocess V— Review and Reset (Progress Assessment)

Introductory Comments

This is in the home stretch of the benchmarking process. The preparation has been done. The decisions have been made. The implementation has been started. It is now time to take stock of progress and prepare for the next round of the benchmarking process.

STEP 13
Review Benchmarking Integration

You need to review how well your organization has been able to integrate the benchmarking tool into the fabric of its

Benchmarking

goal-setting and management system. This step is the last of the process steps which are unique to benchmarking. You should ask yourself several questions.

- Have you included an appropriate level of ongoing benchmarking into the plans developed in Step 11?
- Has management bought into benchmarking as a valuable part of its planning activities?
- Is benchmarking planning included in all managers' performance plans?
- Have the technical experts accepted benchmarking as a way to generate improvement ideas that complement their own?
- Has a satisfactory benchmarking process been deployed broadly throughout the entire company or organization?
- Has the expected (or promised) level of benchmarking ROI been delivered?
- Has commitment and enthusiasm for benchmarking spread throughout the organization, not just among the benchmarking facilitator specialists?
- Are benchmarking skills spread widely throughout the organization?
- Is there a feeling of ownership and pride on the part of benchmarking teams?
- Are the benchmarking facilitators committed to such an effective deployment that their own jobs will disappear?

If the answer to all (or most) of these questions is "yes," you are well on the way.

STEP 14
Assess Project Progress and Update Goals

In addition to reviewing the benchmarking acceptance, good project management involves monitoring of the implementation plans of Step 12. This assessment should involve a few highly indicative and visible metrics which clearly show progress. Those metrics should be summarized at key schedule checkpoints. They should be reported to management, the implementation team, and others with a need to know. The monitoring and reporting should continue after implementation is complete to assure stability and achievement of longer term goals.

If the monitoring indicates a problem in attaining results on schedule and at planned cost, corrective action should begin as quickly as possible. If the implementation is going exceptionally well (or even as planned on a challenging project), consideration should be given to appropriate recognition and rewards.

This assessment also tracks progress toward the benchmarking goal of becoming best at everything you do. Camp calls this "leadership maturity." It is reached when best practices are implemented and institutionalized throughout your organization's plans, processes, products, and services. What are some of the tests for leadership maturity? You might ask yourself:

- Do all your benchmarking key measurements demonstrate good gaps when compared to the best organizations?
- Are other good companies calling (i.e., benchmarking) you?
- Are your customers completely satisfied (or even delighted) with your products and services?

- Are knowledgeable experts and your customers recommending you to their peers and colleagues?

If answers to these questions are overwhelmingly affirmative, then you have made progress and should be in an excellent competitive posture. Even so, remember that leadership achieved is not necessarily leadership retained.

Incidentally, when other good companies start benchmarking you, that is a wonderful opportunity for two-way, mutually beneficial exchanges of information. Much of this benchmarking process still applies. However, you need to modify the process somewhat when someone else initiates the benchmarking. For example, Step 5, "Choose Your Benchmarking Partners," diminishes to doing some research on the organization that wants you for a partner.

STEP 15
Reset Goals and Return to Step 1

Periodic updating and resetting of goals is needed to assure that leadership is reached and maintained. This step provides awareness of changing conditions, helps continuous improvement, and leads to benchmarking maturity. It creates a high probability that your data and assumptions are current and valid, and that you continue on the road to becoming best at all your activities.

Recalling the earlier "shooting at a flying duck" discussion, resetting goals and looping back for another round of benchmarking helps validate your prior projections and alerts you to new competitive threats. This author's experience is that goals are almost always reset to a more challenging level. Lowering goals is usually an admission of failure (unless unachievable goals were initially set). Challenging goals which force you to consider unconventional (non-bus-

Chapter 11: Subprocess V—Review and Reset (Progress Assessment)

iness-as-usual) improvements often lead to the pleasant surprise of attaining the goal ahead of schedule. Thus, you can set new challenges sooner than expected for continuous improvement.

When you loop back and repeat a disciplined benchmarking process like the one proposed in this book, it is usually easier each time around because you have learned and set a foundation. But experience cautions against the following temptations:

- Do not let your vigilance down after some initial success.

- Do not assume that last time's best companies are still best—check it.

- Do not take shortcuts by looping back to Step 7 (or elsewhere within the process); go all the way back to Step 1 and consider the need for doing each step.

- Do not defer ongoing benchmarking unless you have given it due consideration and made a conscious decision that it will not provide ROI benefits to your organization at this time.

There are no hard-and-fast rules on the frequency of benchmarking, nor on the size of the effort for each round. It all depends on a number of circumstances including: bad gaps between your organization and benchmark and/or total customer satisfaction; resources available; anticipated resource requirements, etc. Because most organizations budget and plan on an annual basis, it is desirable to factor an appropriate level of benchmarking (for processes at all priority levels) into the annual plan. Camp suggests (and this author wholeheartedly agrees) that if the next significant benchmarking is deferred for three years or more, so much will have changed that the benchmarking team should start from scratch. Otherwise, one round of benchmarking can be a springboard for the next (with some of the cautions mentioned earlier).

This author advises that appropriate levels of benchmarking truly be ongoing and continuous. My premise is that if the best decide to rest, they will soon be eating someone's dust.

Chapter 11: Subprocess V—Review and Reset (Progress Assessment)

SOME THOUGHT STARTERS!

1. How often are plans updated in your organization? How can plans be updated to reflect an appropriate level of ongoing benchmarking?

2. Has your organization noticed an increase in the number of incoming calls asking for information about your processes? What does (or would) such an increase mean?

3. When goals are reset, are the new levels consistent with the organization's long-range strategy? What is the ultimate goal? Is it realistic?

12/Some Possible Inhibitors

Introductory Comments

For organizations just getting started in benchmarking, it is helpful to be aware of some of the more common inhibitors and pitfalls. Some of these inhibitors will completely kill a benchmarking effort (although it is usually "deferred indefinitely"). Others will make the activity less than fully effective and/or overly costly. No one company or organization is likely to experience all these inhibitors, but almost all will suffer through some of them.

Many of the following ideas have been touched on in earlier chapters. This chapter will bring them all together for more ready access to the reader.

Getting Top Management Support

Support from *all* levels of management is needed to make benchmarking activities successful. But top management support is critical to make the benchmarking tool a part of the organization's culture. In most organizations, enthusiastic and clear support from the top tends to permeate downward through the management ranks.

IBM Rochester was blessed to have top management support for benchmarking. Site General Manager Larry Osterwise understood its part in the Malcolm Baldrige National Quality Award criteria. He was there in 1989 when the benchmarking deficiencies were discovered by the assessment team and corroborated by the MBNQA examiner visit team. Osterwise supported the assignment of a senior technical person to define and fix the deficiencies. He supported that individual's requests to his senior staff for information, Benchmarking Council representatives, education, etc.

If your organization does not have this top level support, the following are some suggestions to cultivate it:

- Get some influential person in your company or organization to become a knowledgeable benchmarking champion. That person can start advising management of needs and benefits.

- The benchmarking champion can point out the need for benchmarking in the MBNQA criteria (or in any other comprehensive Total Quality Management system).

- The champion can research some documented benchmarking success stories pertinent to your organization and relay them to top management.

- The champion can also do some local analysis and suggest some areas of the organization that could benefit most from benchmarking.

- The champion can recommend a means of promoting and enabling effective benchmarking (possibly a facilitator, a network into "the trenches," and some training and education).

Prioritizing What to Benchmark

Because the goal is to continuously improve to become best at everything you do, then everything you do is a target for benchmarking. As a result, prioritizing what to benchmark becomes one of the most critical—and potentially troublesome—steps in the process.

How is this prioritization to be done? As mentioned earlier, it is very much a function of the local circumstances. But the following are some very important questions to ask about activities (work products) under consideration for benchmarking.

- Is this work product the cause of customer dissatisfaction (especially external customers)?

- Is it a cause of management concern and attention? Is there any reason to believe that someone "else" may be doing this a lot better than you are?

- Is your current performance on this work product a long way from where you would like to be?

- Is this a very important (i.e., critical) work product in the context of all you do?

- Is this work product making you non-competitive?

- Is there reason to believe that a relatively small investment in this work product could pay huge dividends?

If the answer to any or all of these questions is "yes," the work product should probably be a high priority target for benchmarking.

Benchmarking Justification Through ROI Analysis

Coming up with a compelling ROI justification for a proposed benchmarking activity is frequently very difficult. The first reason is that estimating the investment needed is difficult until you have had a few benchmarking experiences under your belt. Second, it is difficult to segregate the resources invested in benchmarking because many activities (8 of the 15 process steps) are not unique to benchmarking. Of the seven unique benchmarking process steps, the benchmarking teams usually intersperse most of them with other duties and thus do not have an accurate sense of what expenses are to be charged to benchmarking. Similarly, the net performance gains made in the key benchmarking metrics are usually attributable to several improvement changes, some of which resulted from the benchmarking and some of which did not. Thus, ROI computation often becomes a matter of "best guesstimates."

If a verifiable ROI calculation is needed, it must be carefully defined and computed. The measurement verification must be done by an explicit set of rules, guidelines, and assumptions. A financial analyst's help is often needed to set up definitive ROI measurements.

This author has no experience with a definitive ROI on a particular benchmarking activity, but he has participated in some ROI "best guesses." The process becomes analogous to computing ROI on your organization's investment in employee education.

How to Get Started

One of the most frequently asked questions about benchmarking is "How do I get started?" There are several key considerations. You do not quasi-randomly select a benchmarking target process. Nor do you select a benchmarking partner that you have heard a few good things about and/or that you have easy access to because your brother-in-law works there. (Alas, this does happen on occasion.)

Instead, you first familiarize yourself with the benchmarking process (and enlist the help of a local benchmarking facilitator if you have one). Then you assign a knowledgeable person or small team to do the benchmarking and you give them the time and resources to do a credible job. Subprocess I, Self-introspection, and Subprocess II, Pre-benchmarking, are next. Now you are ready to do what most people think of as benchmarking—the actual data collection.

Determining Appropriate Benchmarking Measurements

This topic was covered in some detail earlier in this book. To summarize here:

- Assure that the selected measurements are important.

- Assure that they are non-confidential (or draft a formal non-disclosure agreement with the benchmarking partner).

- Assure that many (if not all) of the measurements pertain to customer satisfaction and quality.

- Assure that the measurement is not so tuned to your current process that you cannot understand someone else who uses a different (and maybe better) process.
- Assure that the measurement is one that you would be willing to share if your benchmarking partner asks about your achievement level.
- Assure that sharing the measurement information is legal and ethical.

As a final check of your benchmarking measurements, ask yourself, "Would my company/organization be embarrassed if the local newspaper reported that I am sharing this information with my benchmarking partner?" If the answer is "yes" or "maybe," think about it some more—and maybe talk to your legal department, too.

Fear of Breaking Company Security Rules

Sensitivity and confidentiality of data can be a difficult aspect of benchmarking. Many good benchmarking activities do not involve the sharing of confidential data. If sensitive data must be shared, a non-disclosure agreement should be drawn up and signed by both parties before the sharing begins. Sometimes your organization's Legal Counsel or Purchasing group needs to review and approve.

If confidential data is not to be shared, several pointers can be summarized here. First, generating the list of questions you would like to discuss and sharing the list with your benchmarking partner in advance gives you both the opportunity to check out and clear any potentially sensitive areas. Check your list with your management and/or your legal department before sending it to the partner. It is also a good idea to share it with your purchasing agent if your benchmarking partner is a supplier, and with your sales representative if your partner is a customer. These folks can alert you to any particular sensitivities with the partner organization.

In any benchmarking conversation (via phone, video conference, or direct meeting), the list of prepared questions serves as a guide. However, the conversation usually provokes follow-up questions and thus "deviates from the script." If issues of confidentiality arise in these aside conversations and you think an answer (or question) may be sensitive, the best policy (for both sides) is to be honest and to tell your partner that you feel that you should clear that answer and get back to them. Be sure to follow up with an honest and tactful answer.

Educating Benchmarking Teams

At least one person on every benchmarking team should have received some benchmarking education. That could include taking a class, reading a book, consulting with a benchmarking facilitator/expert, or whatever. To attempt a significant benchmarking activity without some basic benchmarking knowledge is akin to taking a car trip without having learned how to drive. It may well lead to unhappy results.

One way to avoid this pitfall is to include a benchmarking facilitator on your team. However, in most companies and organizations that this author has observed, the benchmarking expertise is spread so thin that the facilitator could not possibly participate in every benchmarking team activity. Nor should (s)he be asked to do the benchmarking for the team. The facilitator does not normally have the in-depth expertise of the process/product/service to ask the right questions, understand the answers, and respond to the benchmarking partner's questions. It is almost always more economical to develop some benchmarking expertise in a subject-matter expert than vice versa.

In short, the easiest way to avoid this potential inhibitor is to send the benchmarking team (or their representative) to a short benchmarking class, or ask them to read a benchmarking textbook.

Communicating and Sharing Plans and Results

Ineffective communication is probably one of the biggest inhibitors to maximizing ROI from benchmarking. It tends to be a bigger problem in bigger companies and organizations, simply because of the scope of the communications challenge.

Good communications can help a group that is just getting started at benchmarking to avoid redundant work. Find out if anyone has done what you want to do. If some other group has plans for a similar benchmarking project, you could possibly join forces, share the work, develop a common list of questions, and greatly enhance the ROI by reducing investment and possibly increasing the return.

So how can this sharing and communicating take place? There are a number of mechanisms now in use by benchmarking leadership companies. They include:

- A widely accessible data base of planned and completed benchmarking activities.
- Internal company benchmarking conferences (typically twice a year).
- Electronic benchmarking forums (or bulletin boards).
- Benchmarking newsletters.
- Networking among facilitators.

SOME THOUGHT STARTERS!

1. How can your organization's decision makers be influenced to become more pro-benchmarking? Should they be?

2. Are there any good benchmarking success stories—within your organization or not—that pertain to your processes, products or services? Could they be used as a part of the benchmarking justification and ROI analysis?

3. How should your organization "get started" on the next step in your benchmarking integration? What part does education play?

4. Are there some clever ideas in your organization for sharing benchmarking plans and results? How can benchmarking teams overcome their concerns about "giving away" results of their hard work to others? How can you convince your management that explaining benchmarking activities to others is time well spent?

13/An IBM Rochester Gap Analysis Example

Introductory Comments

Now that the topic of benchmarking has been described in some detail, an example of its actual deployment will be helpful. Several IBM Rochester benchmarking experiences were considered for discussion in this book. The author finally decided to describe an example which includes aspects of a rather straight-forward benchmarking methodology (as discussed elsewhere in this book), but which also exhibits some rather creative ideas. The creativity exemplifies how a team can accomplish the sometimes difficult early steps of the process. The tasks of determining a meaningful set of process measurements, then using those metrics to evaluate themselves and world class benchmarking partners to form a gap analysis are the heart of this example.

The CIM Example

Computer Integrated Manufacturing (CIM) was one of the first areas at IBM Rochester to employ the Analytical Hierarchy Process (AHP) and Maturity Index technique to do benchmarking. While the example comes from a manufacturing environment, the methodology can apply equally well to development, service, and other functions.

The Analytical Hierarchy Process is described in Thomas L. Saaty's 1988 book "Decision-Making for Leaders: The Analytical Hierarchy Process for Decisions in a Complex World." (This tool has accompanying computer software.) The AHP methodology is an organized way to define and prioritize descriptive characteristics of a complex process, product, or service.

Once the characteristics were determined using the AHP, the benchmarking team developed a Maturity Index (MI). This index described several levels of maturity (or implementation progress) for each of the characteristics from the AHP work. Together, the Maturity Index and the AHP characteristics became the quantifiable measurements which were applied to our own local process evaluation, as well as to the operation of several world-class benchmarking partners. A gap analysis was performed on the differences in maturity for each characteristic between the partner organization and IBM. Conclusions and action plans could be formulated from the gap analysis.

Several other IBM Rochester processes are also using this methodology. While it is still being refined, it is considered by these user groups to be very valuable in their benchmarking journey. Clearly, it is only one of many ways to employ benchmarking gap analysis for improvement planning.

Hopefully, it will be helpful to others and stimulate further creative thinking.

The Analytical Heirarchy Process (AHP)

While this author lays no claims to expertise in AHP (and the accompanying software), he has talked at length to local users. This author gratefully acknowledges the work of fellow IBM employees Dick Bouquet, Hank Eyrich, and their AHP team for the following example. The figures and tables used here are their work.

AHP is a structured way to use consensus of subject-matter experts on a particular process (or product, service, etc.) to build a prioritized list of characteristics for the process under consideration. There are three major AHP activities.

A small group of folks who are knowledgeable about the process is assembled. The first activity is to build the hierarchy of defined characteristics of the process. As shown in Figure 12, the group first builds consensus on an overall Level 0 goal for the process. They then proceed to divide that overall goal into a few Level 1 subgoals or business objectives. Those subgoals are, in turn, divided into Level 2 sub-subgoals (called options in this example). Note that the interrelationships of Level 2 options with the Level 1 objectives can become somewhat complex. Any one option can be related to more than one objective. Also, the options can be broken down into Level 3 characteristics and so forth. This hierarchy can become as detailed as the user wishes (the software has limitations on the number of levels, but those limitations are usually no problem at all). As always, common sense must prevail to determine how many hierarchical levels the user group wishes to define and use. The IBM Rochester CIM team found four levels to be adequate.

Benchmarking

Figure 12. AHP Hierarchy of Defined Characteristics

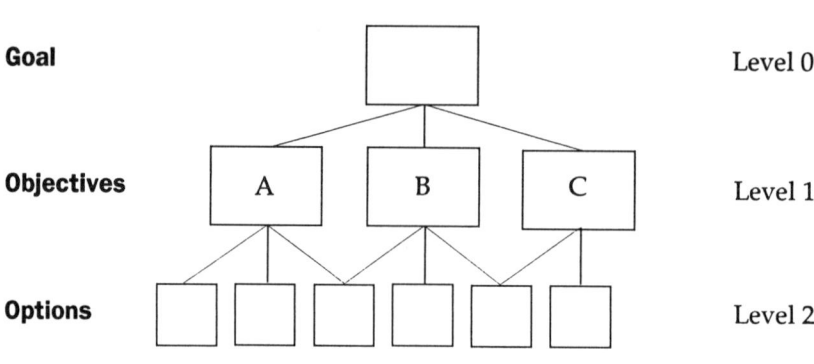

Doing pairwise comparisons is the second AHP activity. This sets priorities by giving relative weights to the defined characteristics within each hierarchy level. It is done by a consensus method based on the judgment of the subject-matter experts. Table 2 uses the Level 1 subgoal objectives from Figure 12 to illustrate this activity.

Consider Objectives A, B, and C. Form a matrix as shown in Table 2. The expert team reaches a consensus (by whatever means they wish) that Objective A is three times more important than Objective B. So a 3 is placed in the matrix row 1, column 2 at the intersection of Objectives A and B.

Table 2. AHP Pairwise Comparisons and Synthesis

	A	B	C	Normalized Average
A	1	3	6	0.65
B	1/3	1	3	0.25
C	1/6	1/3	1	0.10

(This naturally puts a 1/3 weighting in matrix row 2, column 1.) Similarly, Objective A is deemed by the team to be 6 times more important than Objective C. So the matrix element at row 1, column 3 (and at row 3, column 1) are filled in. Also, Objective B is thought to be 3 times more important than Objective C so row 2, column 3 (and row 3, column 2) are known. Naturally, each objective is considered simply to be as important as itself, so the matrix major diagonal is all "ones." The relative importance factors may be integers 1 through 9. Thus a consensus of experts have produced the pairwise comparisons matrix.

The third AHP activity (also shown in Table 2) uses the computer software to convert the pairwise comparisons matrix into normalized averages (or relative weightings). "Normalized" simply means the sum of all the relative weightings equals 1.0. The Table 2 right-side column indicates the normalized weights for the pairwise comparison matrix at its left side. This computation synthesis could, of course, be done manually. The software package also does some other nice things. For example, it checks for inconsistencies in your pairwise comparisons matrix. If a logic inconsistency arises, the software calls attention to it. This is especially useful in larger matrixes in which inconsistencies would not be so obvious as they would be in the preceding simple example.

Figure 13 shows an actual CIM hierarchy with relative importance weightings as determined by the expert panel. Note that adding the weightings horizontally for Levels 0, 1, and 2 produce normalized results. The Level 3 (characteristics) weights for each column (or option) add up to the column header option weight. Thus, the sum of all characteristics weights is also one. (Some of the characteristics abbreviations may be unknown to the reader, but are not necessary to understand the example.)

The Level 3 CIM characteristics from Figure 13 are ranked

Benchmarking

Figure 13. CIM Hierarchy Example

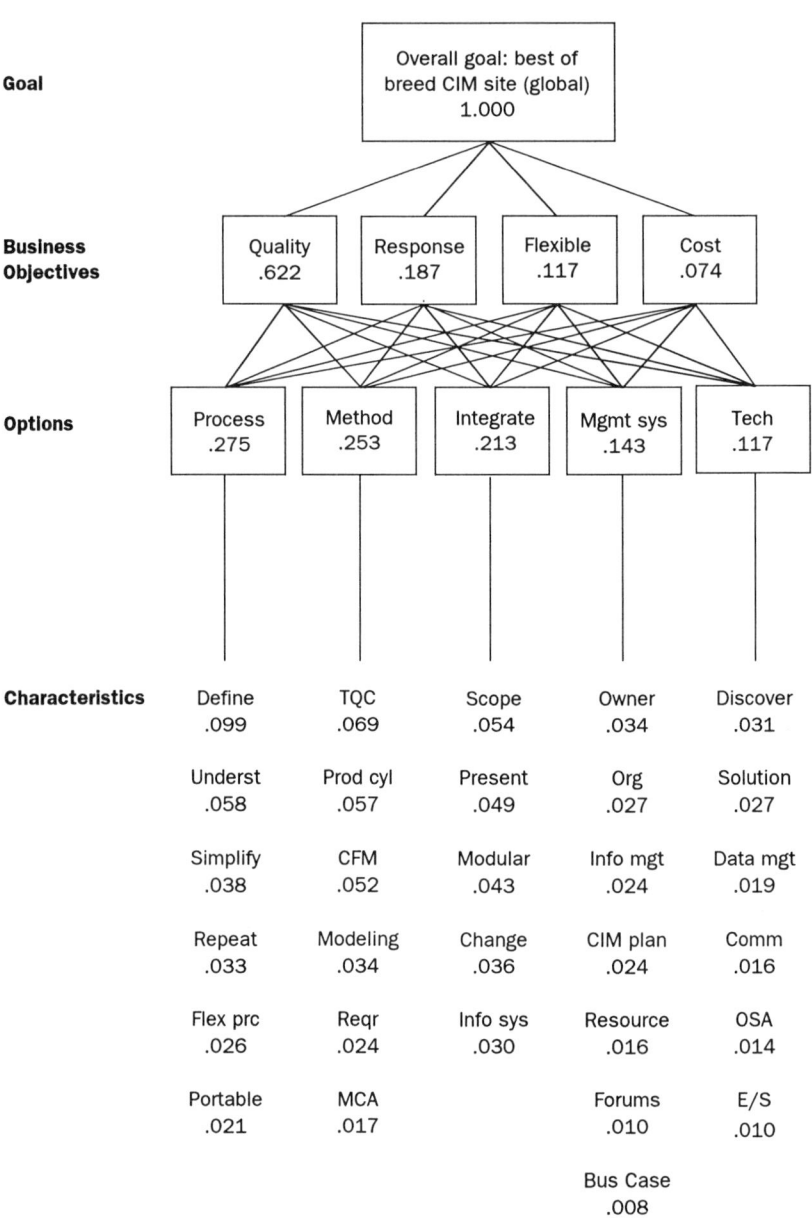

in a Pareto chart format in Figure 14. This illustrates more clearly that the "process definition" characteristic under the "process" option is considered to be the most important characteristic as determined by this team of experts.

Now the CIM team had determined a prioritized set of key characteristics against which they wish to evaluate themselves and compare themselves to best of breed CIM companies. The next step was to develop a CIM Maturity Index.

The Maturity Index (MI)

Now that the group has defined the important characteristics of its process, they must turn them into metrics (i.e., measurements). This can be accomplished by forming another matrix called a Maturity Index (MI). This is a concept that has been used in other applications for several years. Characteristics are listed down the left side to define the rows in the MI matrix (in Figure 15). Across the top (column headers), a few maturity (or achievement) levels are defined. The Rochester CIM group chose five levels starting with None and proceeding through Awakened, Enlightened, Wise, and on to Mature.

Now the task is to determine criteria (or definitions) for each characteristic at each maturity level. This need not be terribly difficult nor sophisticated. Figure 16 gives an example used by the CIM group. The key was to define these maturity levels such that any CIM group could be reviewed and placed at an appropriate level for each characteristic.

There are actually two philosophies for defining MI criteria. One is a linear scale philosophy in which one decides how many levels to use, defines totally immature (or none) at one end, and defines fully mature (or best you can be) at the other end. Then the intermediate three levels are defined for 25 percent mature, 50 percent mature, and 75 percent

Benchmarking

Figure 14. CIM Characteristcs Ranked by Relative Importance

Define	0.099
TQC	0.069
Underst	0.058
Prod cyl	0.057
Scope	0.054
CFM	0.052
Present	0.049
Modular	0.043
Simplify	0.038
Change	0.036
Owner	0.034
Modeling	0.034
Repeat	0.033
Discover	0.031
Info sys	0.030
Org	0.027
Solution	0.027
Flex prc	0.026
Info mgt	0.024
CIM plan	0.024
Reqr	0.024
Portable	0.021
Data mgt	0.019
MCA	0.017
Commun	0.016
Resource	0.016
OSA	0.014
Forums	0.010
E/S	0.010
Bus case	0.008
Total	1.000

Figure 15. Maturity Matrix

Index / Profile	None 1	Awakened 2	Enlightened 3	Wise 4	Mature 5
Process Define Understand Simplify Repeatable Flexible Portable					
Methodology TQC Prod cyl CFM Modeling Reqr MCA					
Integrate Scope Presentation Modular Change Info sys			Definitions		
Mgmt sys Owner Org Info mgt CIM plan Resource Forum Bus case					
Technology Discover Solution Data mgt Comm OSA E/S					
Total					

mature. The second philosophy is to describe the two extremes as before, then determine the intermediate three levels such that your own process will fall very close to midscale for all the key characteristics. Clearly, this can result in a non-linear scale of definitions, but the advantage is that gap analysis (which is relative to your own process maturity) becomes easier to analyze and score than if your own process ranked very high or very low on a linear scale.

Now, armed with the maturity index definition, you are ready to evaluate yourself, and then evaluate the best benchmark partner organizations you can find. Always evaluate yourself first to test the evaluation methods and refine the MI.

Figure 16. Maturity Index Matrix Definitions

Index / Profile	None 1	Awakened 2	Enlightened 3	Wise 4	Mature 5
Process					
Define	No activity	Individual effort to define—owners not identified	Selected processes defined—owners identified	All key processes defined—owners identified	All processes defined—all owners identified
Understand	No activity	Individual effort to understand specific processes	Selected processes understood	All key processes understood & ranked	All processes understood & ranked
Simplify	No activity	Individual effort to simplify specific processes	Selected processes are simplified	All key processes are simplified	All processes are simplified
Repeatable	No consideration	Starting to consider on an individual basis	Built into selected processes	Built into all key processes	Built into all processes
Flexible	No consideration	Starting to consider on an individual basis	Built into selected processes	Built into all key processes	Built into all processes
Portable	No consideration	Starting to consider on an individual basis	Built into selected processes	Built into all key processes	Built into all processes

Some AHP/MI CIM Results

Figure 17 shows some results from the early IBM Rochester CIM group evaluations. The left two columns are the CIM process characteristics and their relative weightings from the AHP analysis (in Figure 17, the relative weightings were

Figure 17. Early AHP MI CIM Results

Index / Profile Chars	AHP Wt	None (1)	Awakened (2)	Enlightened (3)	Wise (4)	Mature (5)
Process						
Define	0.360					
Understand	0.211					
Simplify	0.138					
Repeatable	0.120					
Flexible	0.095					
Portable	0.076					
Methodology						
TQC	0.273					
Prod cyl	0.225					
CFM	0.206					
Modeling	0.134					
Reqr	0.095					
MCA	0.067					
Integrate						
Scope	0.254					
Presentation	0.230					
Modular	0.202					
Change	0.169					
Info sys	0.141					
Mgmt sys						
Owner	0.238					
Org	0.189					
Info mgt	0.168					
CIM plan	0.168					
Resource	0.112					
Forum	0.070					
Bus case	0.056					
Technology						
Discover	0.265					
Solution	0.231					
Data mgt	0.162					
Comm	0.137					
OSA	0.120					
E/S	0.085					
Total						

– – IBM
····· Company C

normalized within each option category). The dash lines are the average maturity scores of our own IBM process as evaluated by the CIM expert team. A reality check of scores by some other IBM CIM experts validated our results. Their scoring produced a curve quite similar to the dash line.

The dotted lines represent the average scores given by a small team of IBM CIM experts (some of whom were involved in our AHP/MI definition effort and some of whom were not) regarding their perception of Company C's CIM process. Company C is an American company deemed by several knowledgeable CIM experts (not all of whom were IBM employees) to be a world class CIM operation. Our team visited their site, interviewed their people, and toured their CIM area before evaluating them.

One might logically ask "What did this gap analysis tell you?" There were a couple conclusions. One is that Company C is a little better than IBM in some CIM maturity characteristics, but IBM is better in others. We both have room for improvement. Another conclusion is that since we believe that Company C is a world class CIM company, this analysis corroborated our feelings that IBM Rochester is also a good CIM company (and can stand alongside the best of them).

Another way to look at gap analysis is shown in Figure 18. Here a different format is used to compare IBM Rochester CIM processes against seven other companies represented by the letters A through G across the top of the table. Some of the seven are from the U.S. and some are from Japan. Company C is the same American company as in Figure 17.

The two columns on the far left are the same as in Figure 17. The third from the left column gives the numeric value for IBM which was plotted as the dashline in Figure 17. The gap information for the comparison of IBM to each benchmarking partner company was converted to plus or

Chapter 13: An IBM Rochester Gap Analysis Example

Figure 18. Another CIM Gap Analysis

Profile		Wt	Base IBM	Gaps						
				A	B	C	D	E	F	G
Process	Calc	0.275	2.2		-1			-1		
Define		0.360	2.3	-1	-1		-1	-1		
Understand		0.210	2.3	-1	-2				-1	
Simplify		0.141	2.4	-1	-2	-1	-1			+1
Repeatable		0.120	2.0					-1		-1
Flexible		0.094	2.0	-1	-1			-1		+1
Portable		0.078	1.4				-1	-1		
Methodology	Calc	0.253	3.2			+1		+1		+1
TQC		0.272	3.1	-1	-1	+1		+1		
Prod cyl		0.225	3.5			-1	+1			+2
CFM		0.205	3.7	+1		+1	+1	+1	+1	+1
Modeling		0.134	2.8	-1	+2		+2	+2	+1	+2
Reqr		0.094	2.5							
MCA		0.067	2.3	-1		-1				
Integrate	Calc	0.213	2.0							
Scope		0.253	2.3		-1	-1	-1			
Presentation		0.230	2.1	+1						
Modular		0.201	1.8		+1			+1	+1	+1
Change		0.169	1.8							+1
Info sys		0.140	1.7	+1	+1		+1			+1
Mgmt sys	Calc	0.143	2.8		+1		+1		+1	+2
Owner		0.237	2.8	+1	+2			-1	+2	+2
Org		0.188	2.7	+1	+2		+1	+1	+2	+2
Info mgt		0.167	2.4	+1	+1	-1	+1	+2	+2	+2
CIM plan		0.167	3.1	-1	+1	+1	+1	+1		+2
Resource		0.111	3.1		+2		+1	+1		+2
Forum		0.069	3.1		-1	+1	+1	+1		+1
Bus case		0.056	2.0	-1	+1					
Technology	Calc	0.117	2.4		+1			+1		+1
Discover		0.264	3.0	-1			-1	+1		+1
Solution		0.230	2.2	-1	+1				+1	+1
Data mgt		0.162	1.9					+1	+1	+1
Comm		0.138	2.1		+1					
OSA		0.118	2.5		+1					
E/S		0.085	2.1		+1					+1
Total	Calc		2.5	2.5	2.4	2.3	2.3	2.1	2.1	1.7

minus integers. Any gap of less than 0.5 is considered a "small gap" (see Section 9.3) and corresponds to a blank in Figure 18. Minus gaps are "bad gaps" in that the benchmarking partner is more mature than IBM. Conversely, plus gaps are "good gaps" meaning IBM is more mature. Any gap between 0.5 and 1.4 becomes an integer 1, between 1.5 and 2.4 becomes a 2, and so on.

So what does Figure 18 reveal? One thing is that lots of the gap entries are blank or plus/minus one. This says again that IBM Rochester compares well to the world's best CIM companies. Most of the "2" gaps are positive good gaps. A second thing is that no one company appears to be head and shoulders above IBM Rochester. In fact, Company G appears in this analysis to be a little behind. Probably, the most interesting thing is what is learned by looking at horizontal rows of the gaps. Looking at each CIM "option" (i.e., block of rows under process, methodology, etc.), one could conclude that IBM Rochester stands high in management system characteristic metrics. But it needs work in the very important process characteristic metrics as indicated by the predominance of negative (bad) gaps. That certainly helps IBM Rochester to set improvement priorities.

Some Concluding Remarks

This IBM Rochester CIM comparison process is intended to be a helpful example of benchmarking. It is not necessarily "typical benchmarking," but it shows the need for innovation in some benchmarking activities. Also, it clearly does not address the entire benchmarking process described elsewhere in this book. But it does discuss several key benchmarking concerns and demonstrates that using the described process and some creativity within it will lead to valuable results.

Certainly, if your benchmarking activity is blessed to have well-defined, appropriate quantifiable metrics (like defect reduction, cycle time reduction, return on assets, etc.), then you may not need to use an AHP/MI approach. This example was chosen because so many benchmarking activities seem to flounder because of a perceived lack of appropriate measurements.

A second remark on this example is that it is very subjective in some ways. The consensus of experts on the hierarchy (definition of characteristics and their pairwise comparisons) is subjective. So is the formulation of the maturity index. Still, intelligent subjective measurements from knowledgeable people is certainly better than "gut feelings" from an analysis standpoint. Sometimes a technique like this takes us out from among the tall trees (like headcount, return on assets, etc.) to where we can again view the forest.

Finally, this example clearly raises other questions (for which this author doesn't have particularly satisfying answers). One question is "Should an IBM CIM-smart team (consisting of some of the AHP/MI derivation team and some others) be the people who evaluate the benchmarking partner companies?" This author's answer is "Why not?" Possibly a team of CIM experts from the partner company could do a more accurate job if they had the time, if they thoroughly understand the maturity index, and if they could be unbiased in their evaluation. But we are not looking for evaluation precision out to three decimal places here. We want a fair evaluation of the big picture. Other methodology questions could also come up. This author would temporarily assume the role of a professor and issue the challenge: let the student answer the questions and improve upon the methodology.

SOME THOUGHT STARTERS!

1. Are appropriate benchmarking metrics readily available in your organization? If yes, what are they and why are they appropriate?

2. Will your benchmarking teams accept the challenge to be creative and persistent in doing benchmarking? How can those characteristics be encouraged and stimulated?

3. Would an organized approach such as AHP be helpful and effective where you are?

4. How might you adapt AHP to your situation?

14/Summary and Conclusions

Summary

Benchmarking is a process in which a small team of people can help their organization to efficiently travel the journey of continuous improvement to become best of the best. They accomplish this by thoroughly understanding their own processes (or products/services); by finding the world class companies or organizations that do what they do; by learning how well those world class companies perform on key customer-driven measurements; by understanding how those companies accomplish their admirable levels of achievement; and by adapting appropriate ideas into their own processes.

This book summarizes information on how to do effective benchmarking from a local benchmarking process class taught at IBM Rochester, Minnesota. It gives some "what and why" information about benchmarking. It then proposes a sequence of steps (i.e., a process) for doing good benchmarking, and it includes some suggestions on how to get started.

Conclusions

Benchmarking is a powerful tool to help any company in its efforts to become best at everything it does. Properly done, benchmarking is helpful to all involved. Poorly done, the process will result in suboptimal exchange of partial information and will usually be a waste of resources for all involved. Indications of a successful benchmarking project include:

- Benchmark target(s) which, if achieved, will make your process best of the best and/or world class.

- A management commitment to attain those targets.

- A feeling of ownership among the process team and a shared enthusiasm to change current practices in order to implement continuous improvement toward (and beyond) the targets.

- A "good feeling" on the part of everyone involved in the project and confidence that the results will help the organization reach desired performance levels faster than business-as-usual improvements.

- An understanding by all that "best" is a moving target and that benchmarking is a continuous practice which must be institutionalized into the company or organization.

Chapter 14: Summary and Conclusions

Effective benchmarking requires a small amount of up-front investment, but the return on that investment makes it well worthwhile. The preliminary steps of benchmarking pertain to good process management and definition of appropriate measurements. This activity should take place whether or not your organization is committed to benchmarking. In addition, good communications with the benchmarking partner organization before/during/after benchmarking data gathering can make your basic process management activities more fruitful and rewarding. Once the activities unique to benchmarking are completed, the process moves on to implementing and monitoring improvement changes. Again, this kind of standard project management should take place whether or not benchmarking occurs. In other words, the tool of benchmarking dovetails very nicely into other management activities. In fact, it cannot be effective if some of those other activities do not precede and follow it.

Thanks to Xerox and others, benchmarking has now become a full-fledged management tool with a formal definition, process, etc. It is the only tool that will tell you when your organization has become "best" because it defines what best is, who is doing it, and (sometimes) how it is done. Instead of asking "Can you afford (the time and resources) to do benchmarking?", perhaps the question should be "Can you afford NOT to be doing benchmarking?"

G.J. BALM

Appendix A

Benchmarking Facilitator Responsibilities at IBM Rochester

- Help Identify High-Potential Opportunities
- Conduct Appropriate Benchmarking Studies
- Maintain a Benchmarking Data Base
- Develop/Teach/Broker Classes
- Be a Benchmarking Competency Center
- Act as a Site Consultant
- Assist IBM Headquarters with Benchmarking
- Communicate Results to Site Liaison Team
- Coordinate Site Contacts to Motorola, Xerox, Others

Appendix B

Benchmarking Rules of Thumb

Benchmarking

1. Never ask your benchmarking partner (i.e., the company or group with whom you have chosen to share information) for information that you would be unwilling to share about your company.

2. If your benchmarking partner is an organization outside your own company, tell them up-front that you do not intend to share any company confidential information with them and ask them that they not share with you any information considered to be confidential by their company (unless, of course, an appropriate non-disclosure agreement document is signed by both parties).

3. If your benchmarking partner is from outside the United States, notify your import/export group (if you have one).

4. If in doubt about confidentiality of any answer to a benchmarking partner's question, then do NOT share the information until after establishing its non-sensitivity or signing a non-disclosure agreement.

5. Assure that your benchmarking partners benefit from their time spent with you. A good benchmarking activity results in mutually beneficial information sharing.

6. Check with your local purchasing department if the company you have selected to benchmark with may be in some sensitive negotiations (or even litigation) with your company.

7. Notify your company's marketing account representative when you benchmark with a company customer.

8. The initial contact with a benchmarking partner organization should be conducted as if it were the start of what will become a long-term friendly relationship.

9. If follow-up contact after a site visit is deemed useful, consider hosting your partner to a reciprocal visit to your site.

10. Remember that no company is best at everything it does. Just because some other benchmarking team has determined that a particular company is world class at a process related to yours, that does not automatically mean that the same company is "world class" for your process.

Appendix C

Benchmarking Checklist

Benchmarking

❏ 1. I have received appropriate benchmarking information and education through classes, reading, or consultation to assure an effective benchmarking experience and to maximize the probability of an appropriate return on investment of my organization's benchmarking.

❏ 2. I have reviewed and updated my understanding of my process, product, or service which I intend to benchmark.

❏ 3. I have developed an overall benchmarking plan for my area of responsibility.

❏ 4. I have made a significant effort to see if someone else in my company has recently benchmarked a process very similar to mine.

❏ 5. I have investigated what companies (or other parts of my company) are world class in my field of interest.

❏ 6. I have made a significant effort to see if someone else in my company has recently benchmarked with my proposed benchmark partner.

❏ 7. I have selected an appropriate set of measurements (usually customer viewpoint measurements) for benchmarking.

❏ 8. I have informed my site or functional benchmarking coordinator (if one exists) of my benchmarking plan.

❏ 9. I have contacted the local purchasing department to assure that my proposed benchmarking partner company is not one with which my company has requested no unauthorized contact.

❏ 10. I have notified my local purchasing buyer if my benchmarking partner company is a company supplier.

Appendix C: Benchmarking Checklist

☐ 11. I have notified my company sales account representative if my benchmarking partner company is our customer or a potential customer.

☐ 12. I have cleared with management and/or the legal department any potentially confidential or sensitive question that I'd like to ask my benchmarking partner. If it is found to be confidential, I have either generated an appropriate non-disclosure agreement or removed that question from my discussion agenda.

☐ 13. I have generated a clear, concise set of questions I'd like to ask and have shared the list with my benchmarking partner.

☐ 14. I have communicated my understanding of the site visit agenda to my benchmarking partner (if a site visit is planned).

☐ 15. I have included appropriate people on my benchmarking project team to assure proper team expertise and maturity and to smooth the path for implementing changes resulting from benchmarking recommendations.

☐ 16. I have entered my benchmarking process plans and status into a company benchmarking data base (if one exists).

☐ 17. If I am to make a formal presentation to my external benchmarking partners and/or leave an information packet with them, I have had the presentation/packet approved by my management and/or legal department (just as I would for any other external presentation or report).

☐ 18. Upon completion of a contact with a benchmarking partner (especially a site visit), I have sent an appreciation note to that partner.

Benchmarking

❏ 19. Upon completion of my benchmarking activity (or upon reaching some significant milestone), I have updated the company benchmarking data base (if one exists).

❏ 20. Upon completion of my benchmarking activity, I have prepared appropriate documentation (trip report, project report, etc.) so that others can benefit from my team's work.

Bibliography

Books

Camp, Robert C. "Benchmarking: The Search for Industry Best Practices That Lead to Superior Performance," ASQC Quality Press, 1989.

Fifer, Robert M.; Furey, Timothy R.; Pryor, Lawrence S.; and Rumburg, Jeffrey P. "Beating the Competition: A Practical Guide to Benchmarking," Kaiser Associates, Inc. 1988.

Fuld, Leonard M. "Competitor Intelligence: How to Get It—How to Use It," John Wiley & Sons, 1985.

Fuld, Leonard M. "Monitoring the Competition: Find Out What's Really Going on Over There," John Wiley & Sons, 1988.

Juran, J. M. "Juran on Leadership for Quality: An Executive Handbook," The Free Press, 1989.

Saaty, Thomas L. "Decision-Making for Leaders: The Analytical Hierarchy Process for Decisions in a Complex World," RWS Publications, 1988.

Thomas, Philip R. "Competitiveness Through Total Cycle Time: An Overview for CEOs," McGraw-Hill Publishing Company, 1990.

Booklets and Brochures

Kaiser Associates Brochure, "Improving Your Competitive Position Through Benchmarking."

Ibid, "Benchmarking R&D, Engineering, and Other Technical Functions."

Ibid, "Industry Analysis and Competitive Analysis."

Ibid, "The Four Critical Elements of Effective Competitive Management."

Xerox Corporation Booklet. "Leadership Through Quality: Implementing Competitive Benchmarking, Employee Involvement and Recognition—Part I," 1987.

Xerox Corporation Booklet. "Competitive Benchmarking: What It Is and What It Can Do For You," 1987.

Xerox Corporation Booklet, "Competitive Benchmarking: The Path to a Leadership Position," 1988.

Magazine Articles

Altany, David, "Copycats," *Industry Week,* November 5, 1990, pp. 11–18 (reprinted in *Quality Digest,* March 1991, pp. 52–59)

Altany, David, "Share and Share Alike," *Industry Week*, July 15, 1991, pp. 12–17.

Bemowski, Karen, "The Benchmarking Bandwagon: AT&T and ALCOA Share Their Steps to Success," *Quality Progress*, January 1991, pp. 19–24.

Biesada, Alexandra, "Benchmarking," *Financial World*, September 17, 1991, pp. 28–47.

Cook, Brian M., "Terry Rock & Convex Computer: Trying To Be Best in the Business," *Industry Week*, February 18, 1991, pp. 39–46.

Crane, Katie, "Often the Best Nuggets Aren't in the Written Report," *Computerworld*, April 16, 1990, pp. 71–76.

Eyrich, H. G., "Benchmarking to Become Best of Breed," *Manufacturing Systems*, April 1991.

Geber, Beverly, "Benchmarking: Measuring Yourself Against the Best," *Training*, November 1990, pp. 36–44.

Hammer, Michael, "Re-engineering Work: Don't Automate, Obliterate," *Harvard Business Review*, July-August 1990, pp. 104–112.

Hoover, Charles W. Jr., "Return on Investment in Continuing Education," *Chemtech*, June 1990, pp. 338–341.

Layne, Richard, "The Best, The Biggest, and the Debate," *Information Week*, September 18, 1989, pp. 6–12.

McCage, William J, "Examining Processes Improves Operations," *Quality Progress*, July 1989, pp. 26–32.

Other

Commitment-Plus (Newsletter of the Quality & Productivity Management Association), "Benchmarking, The IBM Rochester Way," August 1991.

IBM Class Module Handout, "Measurements/Benchmarking," 1990.

Motorola Course Description, "Benchmarking—BMK 160," 1989.

Index

Analytical Heirarchy Process, 144, 145, 146, 147
assesssment, 127
Baldrige Award, 4, 44, 54, 55, 61, 83, 134
baseline, 20, 108
benchmark, 15
benchmarking education, 139
benchmarking integration, 125
benchmarking team, 53, 54, 58, 82, 136, 139
benefits, 37
breakthrough, 19, 29, 32, 66, 70, 110
change, 10
change management, 115
checklist, 170–172
competency center, 40
competitive analysis, 7, 20, 84
confidential data, 57, 137, 138
cost, 38
crisis, 10, 116
customer satisfaction, 2, 3, 29, 73, 80
database, 52
data collection, 74, 107, 137
defects, 3
definition, 8, 15, 16, 17
education, 53, 134, 139
entitlement, 20, 21
facilitation, 43, 137, 139, 168
focal point, 53–55,
gaps, 20, 29, 74, 100, 107–109, 129, 155, 156
getting started, 137
goals, 116, 119, 127, 128
goal setting, 8, 15
history, 7
implementation, 121, 125
inhibitors, 133, 140
inputs, 72
management support, 49, 134
marketplace, 1
maturity index, 144, 149
measurements, 22, 65, 66, 73, 74, 75, 136, 137,
organization, 8

outputs, 71, 72
partner, 8, 67, 82
prioritization, 27, 80, 135
process, xvii, 16, 48, 52, 53, 55, 57, 59, 64, 65, 71, 115, 125, 136
process management, 65, 66, 69, 75
project management, 65, 115, 119, 122, 127
purpose, 116
question list, 138
rationale, 35
reasons, 35
re-engineering, 19, 28, 74

Return-on-investment/ROI, 27, 38, 107, 116, 136, 148, 161
resetting, 128
rules-of-thumb, 166–167
scope, 20
self-introspection, 69
sharing, 140
six sigma, 9
spider chart, 29, 30
targets, 26
Total Quality Management, 4, 47, 134
types, 31–33
warts, 47

Ordering Information

Benchmarking: *A Practitioner's Guide for Becoming and Staying Best of the Best* ...a how-to book for comparing an organization's processes, products or services with the world's best in an effort to discover ways to do things faster, better, and at less cost.

Bulk Quantity Discounts:

Quantity	QPMA Member Discount	Non-Member Discount
1 - 4	10%	—
5 - 24	15%	5%
25 - 99	20%	10%
100+	25%	15%

Price Per Book: $19.95
(Bulk quantity discounts available — refer to pricing chart above)

Name _____

Title _____

Organization _____

Address _____

City, State/Prov. _____ Zip/Mail _____ Phone (___)_____

Quantity _____ (x) $19.95	
Less: Discount (if applicable)	
Plus: Shipping & Handling*	
Total U.S.	

Method of Payment:
☐ Check Enclosed (U.S. Dollars)
☐ Please Invoice P.O. # _____

QPMA is a non-profit association. Our Tax Exempt ID Number is 36-3126135.

* Add $3 for first book and $2 each additional book for shipping & handling.

Source BB01

To place your order IMMEDIATELY, call (708) 619-2909 or Fax (708) 619-3383

QPMA Information

Yes! Send me more information on the following QPMA products & services:

☐ Membership   ☐ *Commitment-Plus* Newsletter
☐ Conferences   ☐ *Tapping The Network Journal*
☐ Workshops   ☐ Regional Councils (Chapters)

Name _____

Title _____

Organization _____

Address _____

City, State/Prov. _____ Zip/Mail Code _____

Phone (___)_____

Source BB01

PLACE STAMP HERE

QPMA Press
Quality & Productivity Management Association
300 N. Martingale Road, Suite 230
Schaumburg, IL 60173

PLACE STAMP HERE

QPMA Press
Quality & Productivity Management Association
300 N. Martingale Road, Suite 230
Schaumburg, IL 60173